ISRAEL
Land of the Bible

Miriam Feinberg Vamosh

Palphot

Haifa

Nazareth

Tel Aviv-Jaffa

Jerusalem

Ashdod

Ashkelon

Bethlehem

Jericho

Beer-Sheba

Haran

Euphrates

Tigris

Babylon

Ur

Eilat

CONTENTS

Acknowledgements:
We are grateful to all those who assisted in the publication of this book: photographers; publishers; The Israel Museum, The Rockefeller Museum, The Tower of David Museum, the Biblelands Museum, Jerusalem; The Nahum Gutman Musem, Tel Aviv; the Israel Dept. of Antiquities; The Holyland Corporation, Jerusalem; The Nature Reserves Authority and other institutions.

Photographers: A. Allon, W. Balke, L. Borodulin, G. Eldar, S. Ginot, T. Glick, I. Grinberg, D. Harris, Hanan Issachar, Y. Lehman, S. Mendrea, R. Millon, Garo Nalbandian, E. Ne'eman, A. Netzer, R. Nowitz, Osku Pukilla, Z. Radovan, A. Shabataev, Duby Tal & Mony Haramati, Y. Sahar, N. Slepak, M. Sokolovsky
Maps & Illustrations: Andromeda , C. Ron, W. Braun.

Graphic Design: Studio Idit Janowski
©Palphot Ltd., P.O.Box 2, Herzlia, Israel

www.palphot.com
ISBN 965-280-102-x

"*The Lord had said unto Abram, 'get thee out of thy ountry and from thy kindred and from thy father's house and unto a land I will shew thee. And I will make of thee a great nation and I will bless thee'...So Abram departed...He took Sarai his wife, Lot, his brother's son, and all their substance that they had gathered in Haran, and they went forth to go into the land of Canaan.*"
(Genesis 12:1-5)

Some four millennia ago, Abraham left his home in the great city of Ur for a land many hundreds of miles away across the Fertile Crescent. With that journey, the curtain rose on one of history's greatest dramas: Abraham and his descendants not only established a new relationship with God, they created a nation, and transformed Canaan into the Holy Land, a land venerated by millions around the world.

The tiny land of Israel—the land of the Bible—owes its incomparable role in world history to its unique geographical setting. Canaan links the northeastern and southwestern extremities of the Fertile Crescent. It is also wedged between the Mediterranean in the west and the great desert in the east. It therefore became the main corridor between the two great kingdoms of antiquity, Egypt and Mesopotamia— the superhighway of the ancient world.

The Patriarchs, Abraham, Isaac and Jacob, and their wives Sarah, Rebecca, Rachel, and Lea, brought forth a large and influential clan. They traveled the length and breadth of Canaan, and kept company with kings and chieftains. They established themselves in places like Bethel, Beersheba, and Hebron, places that still resonate with their memory.

Though the sale of Abraham's great-grandson Joseph into slavery by his brothers signaled a moral low point for the family, Joseph overcame his fate to attain fame and fortune as Vizier of Egypt. When a new Pharaoh ascended the throne, who, says the Bible, "knew not Joseph", he enslaved Joseph's numerous descendants, now known as Israelites.

Moses remembered God's covenant with Abraham, and led his people from Egyptian bondage back to the Promised Land. Scholars identify the Pharaoh of the Exodus as Rameses II, (1279-1212 BCE) and date that pivotal event around the mid-thirteenth century BCE.

Leaving Egypt, the Israelites wandered in Sinai for forty years. They received the Ten Commandments, which together with numerous other regulations laid down by Moses forged them into a cohesive community. These laws have formed the basis of Judeo-Christian morality and Jewish practice down through history.

Sometime in the late 13th century, Moses' successor Joshua led the people

People of Israel

6

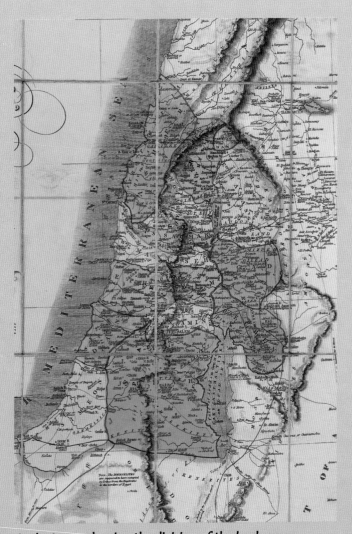

across the Jordan River into Canaan. The next one hundred years were occupied with the settling of the land. Each tribe (descended from Jacob's twelve sons) occupied an area carefully delineated by Joshua. Archaeologists are still searching for concrete evidence of those tempestuous early years, characterized in Scripture by continuous skirmishes between Canaanites and Israelites.

As the period of the Judges drew to a close, around 1020 BCE, the Israelites still had one troublesome enemy: the Philistines. Originating in the Aegean islands, the Philistines had arrived in the land about the same time as the Israelites and eventually gained control of most of Canaan's southern coastline.

The Philistines constituted a threat throughout the time of Samuel the Prophet. Samuel exhorted the people steadfastly against the worship of foreign deities, interceding for them with God to save them from Philistine repression (I

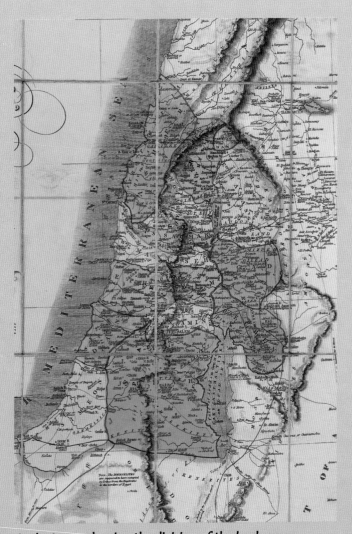

Ancient map showing the division of the land among the Twelve Tribes of Israel

The Holy Land in the time of Jesus

Sam 7). But the people were not willing to rely solely on rituals of sacrifice or the rule of the Judges. They preferred a king. God's choice, according to 1 Sam 9:15-17, fell upon Saul of the tribe of Benjamin.

The two-decade long reign of Saul was characterized by continuous campaigns against the Philistines. It was also marked by battles of a more personal nature for the king, against depression which could be soothed only by the lyre music of a young shepherd boy from Bethlehem. That same boy, David son of Jesse, became the darling of the people after he killed the Philistine giant Goliath. Subsequent rivalry with Saul necessitated David's flight from the king's clutches. When Saul died by his own hand at Mount Gilboa after an ignominious defeat by the Philistines, David ascended the throne of Judah. Eventually, he defeated the followers of Saul's son, Ish-Boshet, to bring the rest of the Israelite tribes under his rule.

In an attempt to unite the quarrelsome tribes, David moved his capital from Hebron to Jerusalem, then known as Jebus. At that time, around 1000 BCE, the city was in the hands of the Jebusites, a Canaanite people. With his conquest of Jebus and his purchase of Ornan's threshing floor—Mount Moriah—where he sacrificed to God and halted the ravages of a plague, David transformed the tiny mountain stronghold into the capital of his nation.

David consolidated territories as far north as central Syria, and finally reduced the ferocious Philistines to vassals of Israel. By 961 BCE, when his son Solomon took power, the expanded kingdom was a major player in international politics. Through hundreds of marriages, Solomon forged alliances

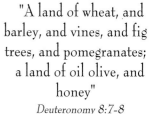

"A land of wheat, and barley, and vines, and fig trees, and pomegranates; a land of oil olive, and honey"
Deuteronomy 8:7-8

with the ruling houses of Phoenicia, Moab, Ammon, and Edom. In his dedication prayer for the new Jerusalem Temple, Solomon calls it *"this place of which thou hast said 'My name shall be there'"* (I Kings 8:29). With extraordinary perception, Solomon recognized the Temple as a place to call upon the name of the God whose spirit dwells in Jerusalem, but whose presence fills the world.

Solomon's wisdom apparently did not extend to certain of his governing activities. His extensive building projects constituted a severe hardship for the people; upon his death in 928 BCE, when the people came to Rehoboam, Solomon's son and successor, to ask that some restrictions be lifted, Rehoboam retorted: *"My father also chastised you with whips, I will chastise you with scorpions"* (I Kings 12:14). In the face of such intransigence, a former overseer of Solomon, Jeroboam, was able to wrest a huge block of territory from the Davidic dynasty. From Jerusalem, Rehoboam ruled the truncated kingdom of Judah, while Jeroboam established the capital of the northern kingdom at Dan. The two kingdoms, Judah and Israel, existed side-by-side, alternately allies and enemies with each other and with their neighbors. Life was harsh; the prophets

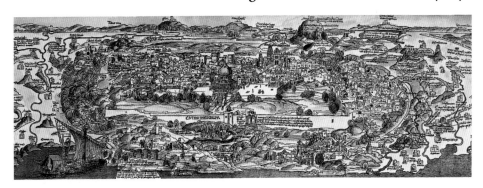

denounced the exploitation of the underclass and idol worship while they warned of impending doom. And indeed, in 721 BCE, the mighty arm of Assyria crushed Israel, exiled the populace and replaced it with its own citizens. Jerusalem was spared destruction when the Assyrian army was felled by a plague at its gates, but in 586 BCE the city and Temple were laid waste by the Babylonians, and most of the people were exiled to Babylon.

The exile of the northern tribes brought about their disappearance as a cohesive group and they became known as the "ten lost tribes". But for Judah, Babylon proved a fertile ground for the revitalization of the faith of the deportees, who around this time began to be known as Jews. Forty-six years later, when the Babylonian Empire fell to the Persians, Cyrus the Great allowed Jews to return to their land. Under the leadership of Ezra the scribe and Nehemiah the prophet, Jerusalem's walls were rebuilt, and sacrifice was reinstated in the

Temple, restored in 519 BCE.

In 332 BCE Alexander the Great swept through the lands of the Near East, introducing the peoples of the region to Hellenism. Each conquered people adapted the new Hellenistic faith to their already existing creeds, but among the Jews there were many who remained true to the worship of one God.

The Jews chafed under heinous restrictions placed upon them by Alexander's successors, the rulers of Palestine and Syria known as the Selucids. Finally, revolt broke out under the leadership of Judah the Maccabee. The revolt culminated with the liberation of the Temple from pagan hands (commemorated by the festival of Chanukah).

Judah's brother Jonathan became the first sovereign of the Hasmonean dynasty, which continued to rule an ever-expanding kingdom until political intrigues and corruption took their inevitable toll. The land was ripe for invasion, and Rome, the ascendant power in the region, took the land in 63 BCE renaming it Palestine.

Flowers
of
Israel

10

Detail from Titus' Arch in Rome, showing the Jews being taken into exile

Rome ruled Palestine through the offices of local client-kings. Judea's sovereign was Herod the Great, who, with the generous backing of Mark Anthony and Octavian took power from Antigonus, the last prince of the fatally-weakened Hasmonean house.

Herod brought fame and fortune to his kingdom with his colossal expansion of Jerusalem's Temple, and construction of the Caesarea port, one of the busiest in the Mediterranean. But he ruthlessly hounded his enemies, real and imagined. Luke's account of Herod's murder of the Holy Innocents in Bethlehem is typical of his cruel and vengeful character.

When Herod died after thirty-five years on the throne, his son Archelaus succeeded him in Judea and two other sons, Philip and Antipas, in the northern territories. Archelaus, however, proved so inept that the Romans replaced the Herodian dynasty in Judea with direct rule by governors who plundered the country for their own gain. People yearned for freedom, and messianic fervor reached new heights. In 66 CE, a revolt broke out that the Romans were unable to contain. In 70 CE, the Temple was destroyed. Some three years later, the last of the revolutionaries died at their own hands, surrounded by thousands of Roman legionaries, in the wilderness fortress of Masada.

Afterwards, despite restrictions, the Jews took up the threads of their lives. But only 60 years later, rebellion reared its head again, under the leadership of one whom many believed to be the Messiah, Bar Kokhba. In 135 CE, this uprising, too, was furiously crushed by Emperor Hadrian who exiled all Jews from Jerusalem and Judea.

Into the maelstrom of the Roman era, in around 4 BCE, Jesus of Nazareth was born. Jesus' teachings of a return to a purity of faith and actions, and the numerous healing miracles he performed during his three-year public ministry brought him many followers, but also earned him his share of enemies. His actions finally came to the attention of the Roman authorities and Pontius Pilate ordered Jesus' execution, which was carried out during Passover, 33 CE.

On foundations laid by Peter and Paul, converts to the new faith were made throughout the world. But Roman oppression forced adherents of the young faith to go underground. Consequently, it was not until the Roman empire itself accepted Christianity, under Emperor Constantine in 313, that the marking and visitation of the places sacred to the faith began.

Early in the fourth century, Constantine's mother Helene came to the Holy Land to seek out the sites of central events of Christianity. Churches were soon built in Jerusalem and in Bethlehem. As the new Christian empire expanded, ruled from its capital Constantinople, thousands of pilgrims flocked to holy places throughout the country, many of which are still venerated today.

In the wake of the two Jewish revolts, Jerusalem had been transformed by the Romans into no more than an armed camp. But during the heyday of the Byzantine empire Jerusalem's star shone brightly in its own right, as the scene of Jesus' Passion. The invasion of the Persians in 614 CE, however, brought the Byzantines to their knees. Though the Christian empire weathered this storm, Muhammad had already established his new faith in Arabia, and in 638 an Islamic army conquered Jerusalem.

By the close of the seventh century, the Muslims added their own sacred

Jaffa, with Tel Aviv in the background

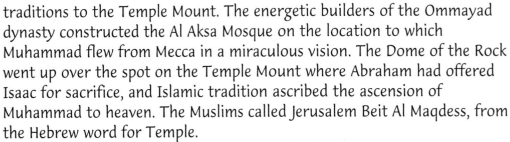

traditions to the Temple Mount. The energetic builders of the Ommayad dynasty constructed the Al Aksa Mosque on the location to which Muhammad flew from Mecca in a miraculous vision. The Dome of the Rock went up over the spot on the Temple Mount where Abraham had offered Isaac for sacrifice, and Islamic tradition ascribed the ascension of Muhammad to heaven. The Muslims called Jerusalem Beit Al Maqdess, from the Hebrew word for Temple.

In the centuries following the Ommayad fall from power, the Muslim ruled the Holy Land from far-away Baghdad or from Egypt. As the Fatimid caliphs of Egypt vied for control of the region against the Seljuk Turks, once more the land had become vulnerable to attack, this time in 1099 by the Crusaders.

For the next two centuries, churches and monasteries flourished. Boatloads of pilgrims disembarked at the lively and cosmopolitan port of Acre and filled the roads to the holy places. Even after the loss of Jerusalem in 1187, and with their holdings much reduced, the Crusaders conducted lucrative trade in the Holy Land, exporting the treasures of the East to Europe. But finally in 1291, Acre, the last Crusader bastion in the Holy Land fell.

The new era, the Mameluke period, was named for a class of servants of the Turkish empire who had gained independence in the region. The Mamlukes immortalized themselves in architecture, and many a structure still to be seen in Jerusalem, Acre, and elsewhere bears the mark of their immutable style.

In 1517, a new Turkish dynasty was founded under Sultan Ot'man. His son Suleiman the Magnificent rebuilt Jerusalem and ushered in the Ottoman Empire, which ruled Palestine until the Turks were vanquished by the British and the French in World War I.

General Sir Edmund Allenby entered Jerusalem triumphantly on December 17, 1917. Palestine, ruled by the British under the mandate awarded them by the League of Nations, entered the modern world.

The late nineteenth and early twentieth centuries coincided with the revival of the biblical imperative to return and rebuild the

ancient land of Abraham. Inspired by the vision of Viennese journalist Theodore Herzl, who turned this age-old desire into a modern political movement—-Zionism—Jews came to Palestine to build a new society.

Scientific research, begun after Napoleon's 1799 incursion, took flight with the late nineteenth-century acitivites of the Palestine Exploration Fund. Tells, those mysterious mounds scattered throughout the country, were now understood to be layer-upon-layer of ancient civilizations. They began to reveal their secrets to an intrepid generation of archaeologist-adventurers.

Sadly, this new surge of energy brought violence with it: Suspicious of the newcomers, Arab inhabitants of the country often attempted to sabotage efforts to settle lands purchased by Jewish pioneers. Unable to control the rising tensions between Jew and Arab, the British returned their mandate to the United Nations.

On November 29, 1947, the UN resolved to partition Palestine between the Jews and the Arabs, and the British prepared to leave. One day after the British departure, on May 15, 1948, the State of Israel was declared, and David Ben Gurion became its first prime minister.

The surrounding Arab nations instantly engaged the tiny country in war, from which it emerged victorious some eleven months later. During the ensuing five decades, many more battles have been fought between Israel and her neighbors. Only in recent years have the parties begun to launch a comprehensive attempt at solving their historic differences at the negotiating table instead of on the battlefield. That effort continues in the hope that in the not too distant future, Isaiah's prophecy will come true: *"They shall beat their swords into ploughshares, and their spears into pruning hooks. Nation shall not lift up sword against nation, neither shall they learn war anymore"* (Isaiah 2:4).

Jerusalem

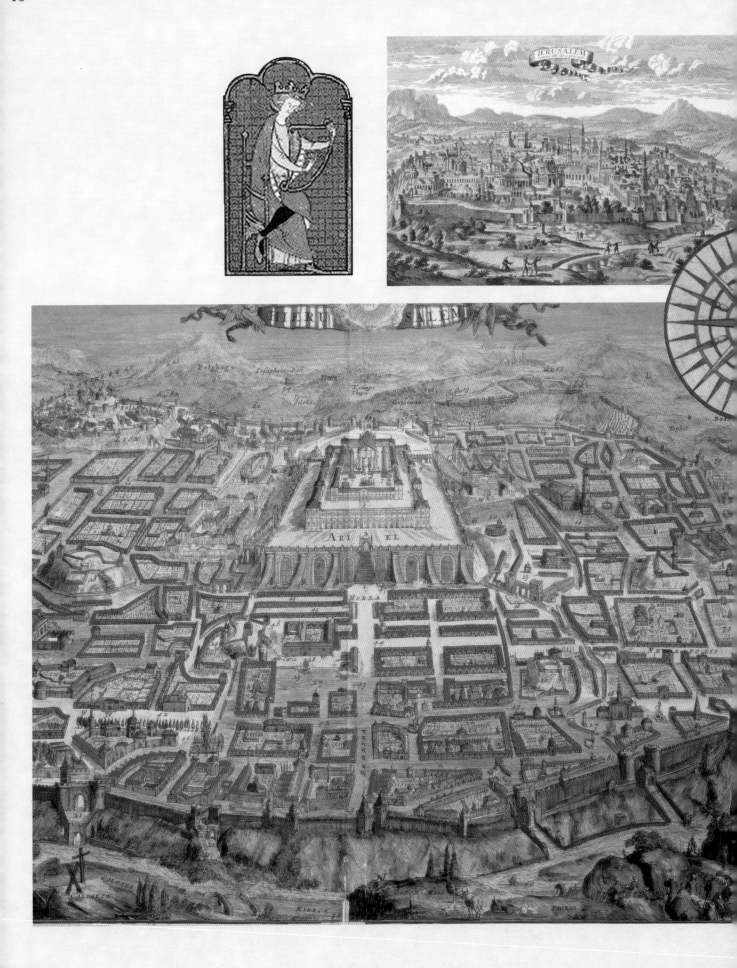

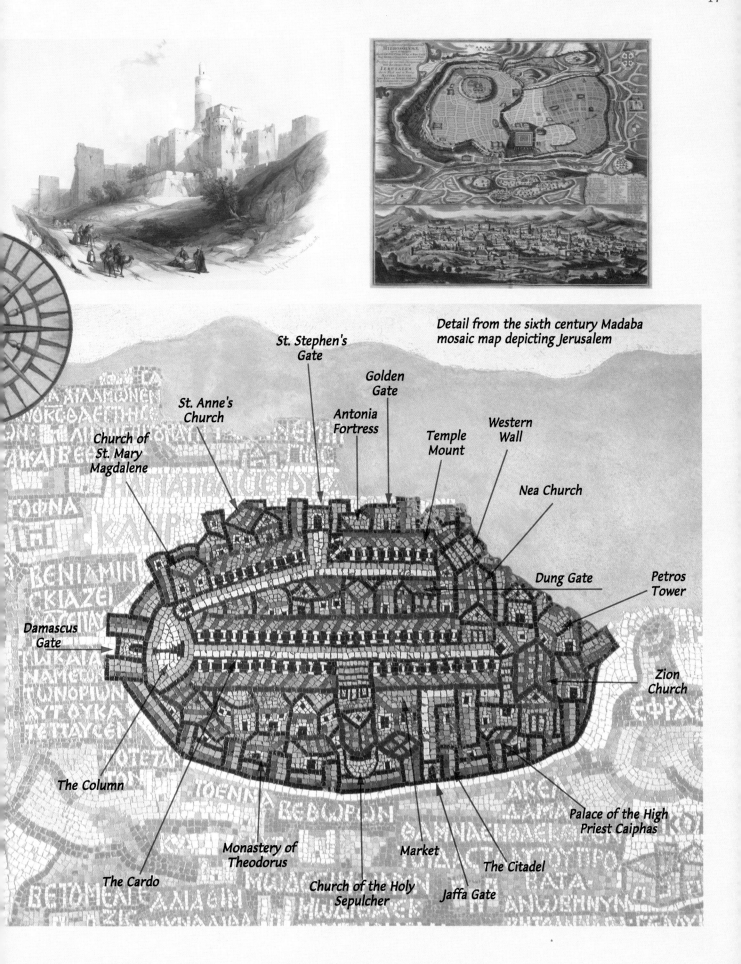

Detail from the sixth century Madaba mosaic map depicting Jerusalem

St. Stephen's Gate

Golden Gate

St. Anne's Church

Antonia Fortress

Temple Mount

Western Wall

Church of St. Mary Magdalene

Nea Church

Dung Gate

Petros Tower

Damascus Gate

Zion Church

The Column

Palace of the High Priest Caiphas

The Cardo

Monastery of Theodorus

Market

The Citadel

Church of the Holy Sepulcher

Jaffa Gate

From Hilltop Fortress to Sacred Capital

"*This is Jerusalem, which I have set in the center of the nations*" (Ezekiel 5:5).

As the mountains are round about Jerusalem" proclaims the psalmist, "so the Lord is roundabout his people" (Psalm 125:2). True to this potent simile, Jerusalem is indeed nestled in the mountainous heart of the Promised Land, equidistant from the wilderness and the sea.

The city that makes its biblical debut when Abraham encounters its king, Melchizedek (Gen 14:18), was first known as Salem. Eventually it was inhabited by the Jebusites, a Canaanite people who rebuffed the efforts of both the tribes of Benjamin (Josh 18:28) and Judah (Josh 15:63) to possess it. Precisely for this reason, King David looked to the mountain stronghold; unpossessed by any one tribe, yet the geographical center of all of them: as capital it would invigorate and unify David's seven year-old reign over the restless and bickering Israelites. Even when the division of the kingdoms brought the rival northern capital, Dan, on the scene,

Jerusalem retained its spiritual centrality, anchored for all time to David's choice of Mount Moriah as the location of the future Temple. It is no exaggeration to say that every event that has occurred in Jerusalem, whether Jewish, Christian or Muslim in character, harks back to David's bold move of his capital from Hebron to the Holy City.

The city prospered during the reign of Solomon, builder of the first Temple, and the kings of Judah. Walls went up to enclose burgeoning new quarters, inspiring the Psalmist to describe Jerusalem as "a city that is closely compacted together" (Psalm 122:3).

But Jerusalem was no stranger to invasion. In one famous incident in the early tenth century, Pharaoh Sheshonk, or Shishak as he is known in the Bible, attacked and "carried off the treasures of the Temple of the Lord and the treasures of the royal palace...including all the gold shields Solomon had made" (1 Kings 14:25). Threats to the city from the great powers surrounding it continued in the ensuing years, presaging the final fall of Jerusalem to the Babylonians in 586 BCE.

Even devastated of most of its population, the worship of the One God was never forgotten. At a burial site from this period, overlooking the Hinnom Valley, an amulet was found inscribed with the priestly blessing: "The Lord bless thee and keep thee, the Lord make his face shine upon thee and be gracious unto thee, the Lord lift up his countenance upon thee, and give thee peace" (Numbers 6:24-25). When the Temple was rebuilt in Herod's day the city knew such glory that the rabbis praised it with the words "eight measures of beauty were given to the world; seven were taken by Jerusalem and one for all the rest".

Jerusalem, a magnet for Jewish pilgrims in the Hasmonean and Herodian eras, continued to be so under both Cross and Crescent. The Crusader order of the Templars protected pilgrims to the Holy City from their headquarters on the Temple Mount, while the Hospitaller Knights saw to their health and lodging as they made their way to the sacred sites where churches had risen over the ruins of the Byzantine era.

After the loss of Jerusalem in 1187, the Mameluke Turks rebuilt Jerusalem in their image. Mosques, colleges of religious studies, and caravanserais sprang up, the intricately designed polychrome facades of which still grace many of Jerusalem's Old City streets. But later, during the days of the Ottoman Turks, the city seemed to recede from the consciousness of the world.

The modern age set the stage for the rediscovery of the political and strategic importance of the Holy City and for a renewal of the love affair of the western world with the Holy City. During that time, European nations vied with each other to maintain a presence in the Holy City building monumental complexes here, each in their own inimitable style. Today, both ancient and century-old European buildings have combined with some of Jerusalem's more recent architectural endeavors to make Israel's capital a unique blending of the old and the new, one of the most appealing and fascinating cities in the world.

The Old City

*T*he walls of Jerusalem's Old City, constructed from 1536-1539 during the reign of Suleiman the Magnificent, embrace a circumference of about two and one-half miles. Many of its gates retain their original ninety degree-angle entranceways, designed to ward off attack. Some still have the massive iron-plated wooden doors that until the beginning of the twentieth century were shut tight from dusk until dawn.

Although these Ottoman-era walls do not consistently follow the lines of earlier fortifications, archaeological excavation has unearthed foundations of walls dating back to the Crusader, Herodian, and perhaps even the Hasmonean eras.

Each of Jerusalem's eight gates has its own fascinating tale to tell.

The Zion Gate:

This gate is named for its proximity to Mount Zion, located to the south. In

Arabic it is known as "The Gate of the Prophet David", as Muslims would exit Jerusalem from here to visit the nearby tomb of King David.

The Dung Gate:

This gate today provides access to the Western Wall. A gate of the same name, mentioned in the Book of Nehemiah (Neh 2:13), was probably located not far from here. The gate's unusual name is apparently because the city's refuse was thrown out here, where the prevailing southeasterly winds would waft the odors away from the city.

The Lion's Gate:

The only open gate in the city's eastern wall, the Lion's Gate got its name from carvings found on either side of the gate's upper section. Oddly, these carvings represent tigers or panthers, and not lions!

During the Second Temple period, animals intended for sacrifice in the Temple were led in through here, and so it was called the Sheep Gate (John 5:2). Christians also call it St. Stephen's Gate, as it is believed that Stephen was martyred nearby. In the battles for

Jerusalem in the 1967 War, the main entrance of Israeli forces into the Old City was through the Lion's Gate.

Damascus Gate:

In the past this most elaborate and busy of Jerusalem's gateways welcomed important personages arriving from the north.

Beneath the present-day Damascus Gate, excavations have unearthed one segment of a gigantic triple archway constructed in the Roman era, as well as a huge plaza. According to the sixth century Madaba mosaic map, a huge column once stood in the plaza. This is undoubtedly the source of the Arabic name for the Damascus Gate, "Bab el Amud", the gate of the column.

Herod's Gate:

There is no connection between this gate and Judea's most famous king,

except the penchant that locals have for naming gates and other imposing monuments for famed historical figures. The gate is also known as the Flowers Gate.

There is a rosette carving above the gateway that may account for this, but a more likely explanation is the presence across the street of a Muslim cemetery. The word for flowers in Arabic is similar to the word "awakened", the name by which those buried in the cemetery were known-as they slept, according to Muslim tradition, until awakened by resurrection at the end of days.

View of the Golden Gate in 1839, David Roberts

The Gate of Mercy:

Also known as the Golden or the Eastern Gate, the Gate of Mercy, though blocked at present, is one of the city's most celebrated portals. Situated opposite the Mount of Olives with its huge Jewish cemetery, and flanked by a Muslim cemetery, tradition holds that the Gate of Mercy will open miraculously at the end of days to admit the Messiah. The Gate of Mercy figures centrally in the liturgy and lore of medieval Jewish pilgrims to Jerusalem.

The New Gate:

This is the only one of the city's gates that does not form part of Suleiman's original design. The Ottoman Empire in its weakened state at the end of the nineteenth century was unable to refuse European demands, among them improved and safer access to Christian holy sites. In 1889, the Turks permitted the construction of this new gate in the northern wall of the city allowing passage from the newly-built pilgrim hostels of Notre Dame and the Russian Compound, to the city's Christian Quarter.

The Jaffa Gate:

Like many of Jerusalem's gates, the Jaffa Gate received its name from the direction it faces. Pilgrims landing at the port of Jaffa and heading to the Holy City found that this gate provided them direct access to the holy places in the Christian and Armenian quarters of the city.

The Citadel

Courtyard of the Tower of David at Dusk.
Photography: Tal Glick

The citadel courtyard, now the excavated heart of the Tower of David Museum

The legendary Tower of David is one of the most impressive landmarks of the Jerusalem skyline. In spite of its name, the Tower of David was constructed not by Israel's psalmist-king but by Herod the Great, two thousand years ago. Eventually, the massive square tower became part of Turkish Jerusalem's citadel. Now this once-critical element in the city's defenses has been turned into one of the world's most original locations for a museum. In each of the citadel's centuries-old guard rooms, The Tower of David Museum of the History of Jerusalem presents the capital's three-thousand year old history and its significance to the three monotheistic faiths, utilizing an array of models and state-of-the-art visual aides. In the citadel courtyard, archaeologists have unearthed finds from nearly every period of the city's history, adding a striking dimension to this already unique museum. Here too, visitors can attend concerts, a sound-and-light show, and even solve a biblical murder mystery!

Visitors take in Jerusalem from the roof of the Tower of David

Model of Jerusalem in the nineteenth century constructed by Stephen Illes in 1873
Photograph: David Harris

Jerusalem reveals some of its most fascinating details from the top of the ramparts. On a walk beginning at the Jaffa Gate and winding around to the Damascus and St. Stephen's Gates, the city's lively and colorful market stalls and busy streets as well as the domes and spires of churches, mosques, and synagogues, come together in a unique panorama. From the Jaffa Gate, another segment of the walk takes in the Armenian Quarter and ends at the Zion Gate with an inspiring view of the Mount of Olives as ancient sentinels must have seen it.

*S*ome 31,000 people live in the Old City's four quarters: the Jewish, Christian, Muslim, and Armenian. Over the centuries, these quarters have shifted, enlarged, or diminished according to historical circumstance, assuming their present dimensions during the first part of the twentieth century.

The Jewish Quarter

Jerusalem's Jewish Quarter has occupied its present southern location within the walled city since 1267 when a call from the famous sage Nahmanides went out to Jews far and wide to renew the city's Jewish community life that had been interrupted during the Crusader era. Since that time, the Jewish population in the Old City has known ups and downs but by the mid-1860's Jews constituted a majority in the city. However in 1948,

during the War of Independence, the inhabitants of the besieged Jewish Quarter were exiled from their walled-city homes, unable to return until the Six-Day War of 1967 reunited Jerusalem.

With reunification, the Jewish Quarter, largely destroyed in the battles of 1948, was restored. Before construction began archaeologists and historians seized the singular opportunity to explore Jerusalem's past.

Restored arch of the Hurva Synagogue

Excavations on an unprecedented scale have brought some 2700 years of history to light.

The present-day Jewish Quarter is an exciting combination of past and present. Visitors wander along the ancient paving stones of the city's most important Byzantine artery, the Cardo, beneath which they can view remains of ramparts from the time of Jeremiah. Later they can visit modern boutiques situated nearby, ensconced within Crusader arcades. At the base of the immense Broad Wall, Babylonian arrowheads were discovered, evidence of the fateful Babylonian advance that signaled the destruction of the First Temple.

The Rothschild building

Remains of the Tiferet Israel Synagogue

One of the Sephardic synagogues in the Jewish Quarter

Central courtyard of the Jewish Quarter

Views of the Cardo, "Main Street", in sixth century Jerusalem. First Temple-era remains were discovered beneath the Cardo and can be viewed through special "wells" in the street. During the Byzantine era this broad colonnaded street linked the important churches of Jerusalem.

The First Temple-era Broad Wall

Stone table and storage jars in the Herodian Mansion

Remains of the magnificent Second Temple-era Herodian Mansion

The Christian Quarter

The Christian Quarter encompasses churches, convents and other Christian-owned properties surrounding the Church of the Holy Sepulcher. The Via Dolorosa, the traditional route taken by Jesus from the Place of Judgment to Calvary, ends at the Church of the Holy Sepulcher and traverses part of the Muslim Quarter on the way.

At the eastern end of the Via Dolorosa, just inside the Lion's Gate, is the Pool of Bethesda. Remains of this huge Second Temple-era reservoir are revered as the site of the healing of the paralytic, as related by John 5:1-15. Archaeologists have uncovered a site next to the reservoir where pagan healing rites were practiced, (the likely spot for the events described by John). Both the Byzantines and the Crusaders constructed churches over the Pool.

An ancient tradition also identifies this

site as the home of Joachim and Anne, parents of Mary, and marks Mary's birthplace here. In 1140 the Crusaders constructed a large church, the Church of St. Anne, in honor of that event. After the fall of Jerusalem to Saladin in 1187, the church was converted into a madrasa or Muslim college of religious studies. In the nineteenth century it was purchased by the French government and given over to the French Catholic order, the Pe'res Blancs, who maintain the area today.

Interior of the Church of St. Anne

Byzantine arches in the Pools of Bethesda

Crusader Chapel over the Pools of Bethesda, with the Church of St. Anne in the background

The Via Dolorosa
and the Stations of the Cross

First Station: Jesus is condemned to death. **Second Station:** Jesus takes up the cross. **Third Station:** Jesus falls for the first time. **Fourth Station:** Jesus meets Mary. **Fifth Station:** Simon of Cyrene helps Jesus to carry the cross. **Sixth Station:** Veronica wipes the face of Jesus. **Seventh Station:** Jesus falls for the second time. **Eighth Station:** Jesus speaks to the women of Jerusalem. **Ninth Station:** Jesus falls for the third time. **Tenth Station:** Jesus is stripped of his garments. **Eleventh Station:** Jesus is nailed to the cross. **Twelfth Station:** Jesus dies on the cross. **Thirteenth Station:** The body of Jesus is taken down from the cross. **Fourteenth Station:** Jesus is laid in the sepulcher

First and Second Stations: Jesus is condemned to death, crowned with the crown of thorns, scourged, and takes up the cross. These stations are located on the grounds of the Monastery of the Flagellation, built over remains of the Roman`era street.

The Via Dolorosa wends westward. Not far from the first and second stations, it is spanned by an ancient arch known as the Ecce Homo Arch, now incorporated into the Sisters of Zion Convent. When the Sisters of Zion came to Jerusalem in the nineteenth century, they sought a location that was significant in the Passion of Jesus on which to build their convent. What better site than the Ecce

Homo Arch, believed to be part of the "judgment hall" (John 18:28) where Pontius Pilate judged Jesus?

While repairs were being carried out beneath the convent in later years, the sisters came upon an ancient pavement which eminently suited the description of the Lithostrotos (the "stone pavement" of John 19:13) where Jesus was condemned. Although subsequent archaeological research has shown the pavement to post-date the time of Jesus by about one century, most agree that the location is indeed part of the Antonia Fortress or the Praetorium, the Roman seat of government where the trial of Jesus is likely to have taken place.

Portions of the Ecce Homo Arch within the church of the Sisters of Zion Convent

The Lithostrotos

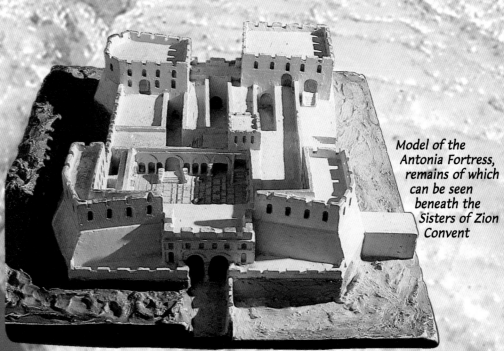

Model of the Antonia Fortress, remains of which can be seen beneath the Sisters of Zion Convent

Third Station: Jesus falls for the first time. A chapel on this site was constructed by the Free Polish Forces after World War Two. Behind it is the center for Jerusalem's small community of Armenian Catholics.

Seventh Station: Located on one of the main market streets of the Muslim Quarter, this Franciscan chapel, rarely open to the public, contains one of the columns that once lined the ancient street.

Crossed arms of Jesus and St. Francis with the Jerusalem Cross, signifying administration of the premises by the Franciscan Order.

Fourth Station: Jesus meets his mother Mary. This station is one of several marked by special paving outside the door of its small chapel and a Roman numeral corresponding to the number of the Station. A bas`relief illustrating the meeting of Jesus and Mary stands over the door.

Ninth Station: Another ancient column, located between the entrance to the Coptic Patriarchate and the Ethiopian Monastery, marks the station where Jesus fell with the cross for the third time.

This grafitti carved on bedrock beneath the Church of the Holy Sepulcher depicts a ship with a broken mast, and the Latin words "Domine Ivimus", "Lord, we shall go up". It may have been carved in thanksgiving for a safe arrival in Jerusalem by very early Christian pilgrims.

Eleventh Station:
Calvary: Jesus is nailed to the cross.

The stone of Unction. On this slab of marble, the body of Jesus was prepared for burial.

Madonna in the Calvary Chapel

Thirteenth Station: Jesus is taken down from the cross.

Holy Sepulcher entrance

Model of the sixth-century Church of the Holy Sepulcher in the Tower of David Museum
Phtography: Yoram Lehmann

Fourteenth Station: Jesus is laid in the tomb. The tomb of Jesus is located in the Rotunda, where Emperor Constantine built his first church in 324 CE naming it Anastasis, or Resurrection. Tombs from the Roman period are visible behind the Syrian Orthodox Chapel west of the Rotunda.

Legend relates that Queen Helene, mother of King Constantine, the first Christian emperor of Rome, ordered the **Church of the Holy Sepulcher** built over a cave where a vision told her she would find pieces of the True Cross. When the queen sent messengers to that locale, they found pieces of the cross which possessed miraculous properties. The church that rose on that site, enlarged and embellished over the centuries, is one of Christendom's and Jerusalem's most renowned monuments. It is uniquely administered by several Christian communities in condominium.

Interior of the Tomb of Jesus

1

2

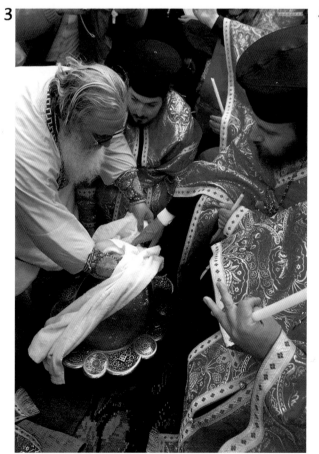

3

4

5

1. Ceremonial unlocking of the Holy Sepulcher doors
2. The Ceremony of the Holy Fire
3. Ceremonial foot washing, part of Orthodox Easter celebrations
4. The Greek Orthodox Patriarch in the Holy Sepulcher courtyard
5. The Syrian Orthodox Patriarch
6. Armenian Orthodox honor guard exiting the church.
7. Ethiopian Palm Sunday celebrations.

6

7

ARMENIAN ORTHODOX
PATRIARCHATE RD.

The Armenian Quarter

The Armenian Quarter is surrounded by its own protecting walls within the Old City, imparting an air of mystery to this section of Jerusalem. Jerusalem has been home for centuries to this community of some 1500 souls, representatives of one of Christianity's most ancient branches.

A historic need for self-defense brought about construction of walls around the Armenian Quarter. Armenia, strategically located between Turkey and Russia, was often threatened by invasion, bringing about the creation of a very tight-knit Christian community there.

After the massacre of one and a half million Armenians in their ancestral homeland by the Turks in April of 1917, survivors sought refuge in the southwestern section of the Holy City, where a small group of Armenian Christians had already lived for centuries.

Scene in the Armenian Quarter

Interior of the Armenian Orthodox Church

Painted pottery, a typical Armenian craft

The Muslim Quarter

The Muslim Quarter of the Old City, the largest and most populous of Jerusalem's quarters, is located in the northeastern part of the Old City. Commerce flourishes on the ground floors of the quarter's buildings, while upper stories are given over to densely inhabited residences. The medieval facades of many Muslim Quarter edifices, with their recessed, semi-domed entranceways, are reminders of the days when the Mamelukes ruled the city. Many of these buildings are now the property of the Wakf, the Muslim religious authority, which rents them to Muslim families.

Tombs of Mameluke notables can be seen behind distinctive interlocking green metal bars, a gnarled ancient fig or tall dark cypress tree revealing their presence. The eye of the observer must be very discerning to take note of these architectural treasures, for the hustle-bustle of the markets supplies constant diversion, with shoppers from far and near conducting a lively give-and-take with persistent merchants.

Ottoman street scene, on display at the Tower of David Museum
Photography: Meidad Sokolovsky

Tamarind juice vendor

42

مسجد

عمر بن الخطاب رضي الله عنه

Mosque of Omar

ممنوع الدخول لغير المصلين

FOR PRAYERS ONLY

Market scenes
in the old city
of Jerusalem

OMAR IBN EL-KHATTAB SQ.

The Temple Mount

The magnificent monuments, stately old trees and lawns of the Temple Mount rise tranquilly above the busy markets in the north of Jerusalem's Old City. From the dawn of monotheism, this place has played a sacred role. Jewish tradition sees it as Mount Moriah, where Abraham offered Isaac for sacrifice (Gen. 22), as well as the center of the world, and the place from which all springs emanate. For the Muslims, this is the third holiest place in the world after Mecca and Medina. They call it Haram el-Sharif, the Sacred Enclosure.

At 740 meters above sea level, the Temple Mount towered above the Jebusite city that became King David's capital. The winds at these heights would certainly have made it the perfect threshing floor, a place to separate wheat from chaff, the function it fulfilled before David purchased it from Ornan the Jebusite (II Sam. 24:16).

Of the magnificent Temple of Solomon that occupied this site, the Bible says "...and the cedar of the house within was carved with knops and open flowers: all was cedar, there was no stone seen...Solomon overlaid the house within with pure gold and so covered the altar, which was of cedar" (I Kings 6). Herod extended Solomon's original Temple platform and expanded the smaller structure built in the sixth century BCE to replace the Temple destroyed

by the Babylonians.

Some sixty years after Herod's Temple was destroyed by the Romans in 70 CE, Emperor Hadrian constructed a shrine to Jupiter here. Byzantine Christianity largely ignored the existence of the Temple Mount, but with the arrival of Islam, a wooden mosque was constructed on the site in 638 CE by Caliph Omar. In 691, the Ommayad Caliph Abd-el Malik Ibn el Marwan built the Dome of the Rock, whose basic form has remained unchanged to this day. A few years thereafter the Al Aksa Mosque was constructed, marking the traditional site where Muhammad arrived in Jerusalem after the Isra, his night journey from Mecca.

Numerous other structures dot the plaza, each with its own tradition. Notable among them is the Dome of the Chain, to the east of the Dome of the Rock; legend relates that on this spot King David judged the people with the help of a chain. If a link in the chain fell while a petitioner was testifying, the king would know the testimony was false.

The Dome of the Rock

The Al-Aksa Mosque

A window in
the Dome
of the Rock

Not everything on the Temple Mount is above ground; beneath the surface are huge vaulted halls were constructed by Herod the Great to support the platform and act as reservoirs.

One of these structures is still known by its old Crusader name, "Solomon's Stables", and has recently been refurbished as a mosque.

Cross-section of the Dome of the Rock on display in the Muslim history room at the Tower of David Museum in Jerusalem
Photography: Yoram Lehmann

View of the rock from which Muslims believe Muhammad ascended to heaven and around which the Dome of the Rock was constructed. At left, a small shrine marks the place where tradition says Muhammad's footprint is to be seen. Some of the numerous columns within the Dome may have previously been used in Herod's Temple

The Western Wall

"This world is like unto the human eye, for the white is the ocean which girds the earth, the iris is the earth upon which we dwell, the pupil is Jerusalem, and the image therein is the Temple of the Lord..." (Bereshit Rabba 63:14)

The Western Wall, or as it is sometimes known, the Wailing Wall, is Judaism's most sacred location. It was, until the archaeological excavations of the modern era began, the last visible remnant of the Second Temple.

Considering its sanctity to the Jewish People, one might think that this massive rampart was at the very least part of the Holy of Holies of the Temple! But to Herod's engineers it represented above all an architectural imperative: to support the arches of the builder-king's massive extension of the plaza on which the pre-existing smaller Temple had stood.

After the destruction of the Temple in 70 CE by the Romans, Jewish sages began to teach that the presence of God, the Shekhinah, never left the Temple. The Western Wall, the only physical reminder of the Temple, became a repository for their spiritual aspirations. When Jews returned here for the first time in the Six-Day War after a nineteen year absence, the Wall, in addition to its enormous spiritual significance, became a symbol of national pride and victory.

"On the eve of the ninth of the month of Ab, when the Jews lamented at the Wailing Wall for the destruction of the Temple, the sound of their weeping would cleave the heavens, and a white dove would appear in the darkness of the night and join the people of Israel in their mourning" (Shir Hashirim Rabba 6:5).

Center: An inscription discovered in the Western Wall excavations, from Isaiah 66:14: "You shall see, and your heart shall rejoice, and your bones shall flourish like an herb". It may have been carved by a Jewish pilgrim in hope of the imminent rebuilding of the Temple.

Scenes at the Western Wall Notes are inserted between the ancient stones, containing the prayers of the faithful.

The Western Wall Tunnel

Massive as it seems, the Western Wall visible at present represents only about ten percent of the remains of the ancient western retaining wall of Herod's Temple platform. The rest is underground, a startling fact first recognized by the nineteenth-century fathers of Jerusalem archaeology, the legendary Titus Tobler, Charles Wilson, and Charles Warren.

In recent years, a tunnel has been dug about 50 feet below ground level, along the entire length of the ancient wall. The tunnel passes beneath the remains of arches of a bridge, Wilson's Arch, first constructed by the Hasmoneans, and replaced in the eighth century. Visitors pass through the tunnel to admire the massive stones of the Temple's Western retaining wall (The

Medieval street built over the remains of an ancient bridge connecting the city to the Temple Mount.

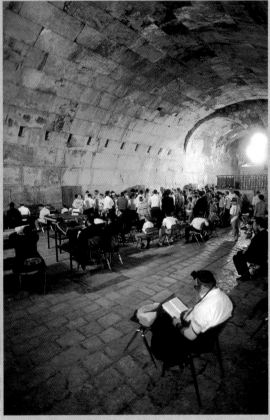

Jews at prayer beneath Wilson's Arch

A Hasmonean-era chamber below the medieval street

estimated weight of one colossal block is 570 tons!). Standing on the two-thousand year-old street that ran parallel to the wall it is easy to imagine it teeming with pilgrims in the days of Jesus.

The tunnel continues past wide trenches that may have been foundations for the Baris, a fortress probably first built by the exiles returning from Babylon in the days of Nehemiah (Neh 7:2) and used by the Hasmoneans who ruled Jerusalem before the Roman conquest. The massive Herodian construction cut not only through these trenches, but also through a pre-existing water system, part of which

later served the Antonia Fortress. The Western Wall Tunnel exits at the Via Dolorosa opposite the Sisters of Zion Convent which stands over the remains of the Antonia Fortress.

The last segment of the Western Wall Tunnel is a water channel.

"Warren's Gate", now blocked, was one of the monumental entrances to the Temple Mount in Herod's day.

The Antonia Fortress

The Holy of Holies rises beyond
the Courtyard of the Women

Royal Stoa and C•
of the Gentiles

One of three towers
built to guard Herod's
Palace, to become known
as the Tower of David

Herod's Temple

"He who has not seen the Temple in Jerusalem has never seen a beautiful building" (Baba Batra 4a). So said the sages of old about Herod's Temple. Herod began expanding the Temple about 19 BCE. First, he doubled the original size of the platform - making it, at about 145 acres, the largest man-made plaza in the ancient world.

He then constructed the Temple in the temenos-style-a- graduated approach to increasingly sacred areas. The outermost plaza, the

Courtyard of the Gentiles led to inner courtyards which opened on to the the Holy of Holies. The Holy of Holies was divided into two sections. In the front, the Golden Candelabra and the Table of the Shew-bread were kept (put on display on the pilgrimage festivals). At the back, behind a curtain—the one mentioned in the story of the Crucifixion of Jesus—was the most sacred part of the Temple, the dwelling place of God's spirit. Only the High Priest had access to this place and only once a year, on the Day of Atonement.

In front of the Holy of Holies stood the altar on which animal burnt offerings, meal, and wine were placed. Hundreds of priests and Levites were kept busy every day of the year with the sacrifices and the upkeep of the precinct (frequented daily by thousands) as well as the administration of the Temple treasury, and levitical musical performances.

According to Josephus, the Temple took eleven years to build, of which three were spent stockpiling the necessary materials. A workforce of ten thousand laborers was employed in the task. Another important source, the Gospel of John, states that the Temple was under construction for forty-six years (John 2:20).

Insets: Scale model of Jerusalem as it looked in Herod's day, on exhibit at Jerusalem's Holyland Hotel

The Southern Wall Archaeological Park

Diorama on display at the Tower of David Museum depicts the Robinson's Arch entrance to the Temple as it must have looked in Herod's day. At left, remains of Robinson's arch jut out from the wall above eighth-century construction in the Southern Wall excavations
Photography: Yoram Lehmann

A Hebrew inscription discovered in the Southern Wall excavations, on a stone that may have toppled from the wall during the Temple's destruction. It reads "to the place of trumpeting..."

Below: Steps ascend to the Hulda Gates as reconstructed at the Holyland Hotel Model of Jerusalem. At right, visitors walk the original steps discovered in the Southern Wall excavations.

The City of David

The fabled Spring of Siloam was Jerusalem's most important water source. Its Hebrew name, "shiloah", is derived from the word meaning "sent", a fact noted in John's account of Jesus' healing of a blind man (John 9:6-12).

The "sending" of the waters of the Pool of Siloam occurred during the reign of King Hezekiah. In 701 BCE, King Hezekiah of Judah took defensive measures against the menace of Assyrian invasion. Among these measures was the cutting of an underground channel to transport the waters of Jerusalem's Gihon Spring from its exposed position beyond the city walls to a reservoir within (11 Chron. 32). This reservoir became known in Second Temple times as the Pool of Siloam.

The city's first water system was probably a shaft dug by Jebusite inhabitants to reach the Gihon spring from within the walls. This shaft may appear in the story of the capture of Jerusalem by David. According to II Samuel 5:8, David ordained that "whoever getteth up to the gutter [the water tunnel] and smiteth the Jebusites...he shall be chief and captain". In a bold move, David's general Joab led his men up this water shaft right into the midst of the Jebusites, taking the city by surprise.

The shaft was first rediscovered by British archeologist Charles Warren, and re-accessed some years ago during excavations by Israeli archaeologist Yigal Shiloh. Hezekiah's Tunnel, where visitors slosh through over 500 meters of thigh-

Hebrew inscription, on display at the Istanbul Archaeological Museum, describing the construction of Hezekiah's Tunnel

The Pool of Siloam

Rock-cut interior of Hezekiah's Tunnel

Remains of channels in the City of David, quarried to deliver water to fields in the Kidron Valley

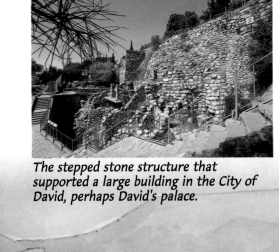

The stepped stone structure that supported a large building in the City of David, perhaps David's palace.

high water to view the evidence of ancient rock quarrying, is one of Jerusalem's most exciting attractions.

At the exit of Hezekiah's Tunnel lies the Pool of Siloam, where ancient column-drums are all that remain of a Byzantine church. The Pool is known in Arabic as Birket Sitnah Mariam, the Pool of Our Lady Mary. According to tradition, Mary the mother of Jesus would come here to wash clothes. The steps that descended to the pool were considered sacred and are mentioned in several pilgrims' accounts.

Artist's rendering of Jerusalem as it looked in Solomon's time.

Mount Zion

Mount Zion is a spur of one of Jerusalem's western hills. It began to be regarded as a separate geographical entity once the walls of Suleiman the Magnificent excluded it from the city's fortified area, the city wall being just to the north of the Mount. On the southeastern side of Mount Zion runs the Valley of Hinnom where in the days of the First Temple child sacrifices were made to the Canaanite fire god, Moloch, and where legend also places the suicide of Judas. Jerusalem's ancient walls probably ran along the edge of the Hinnom valley.

The Cenacle, or Room of the Last Supper

Since the 12th century, pilgrims have identified the Tomb of King David (as well as a now-unknown site for the Tomb of Solomon) on Mount Zion. Although the Bible states that David was buried "in the city of David" (I Kings 2:10)—located at the foot of Mount Zion—it is possible that a reform, including obedience to the dictum not to bury within the city limits, was initiated during the reign of one of the kings of Judah. Perhaps at this time, the remains of David and other kings were re-interred on this hill overlooking David's city.

The Last Supper, as well as the dramatic events of the first Pentecost after the Crucifixion—the speaking in tongues—are also said to have taken place on Mount Zion. Both the Tomb of King David and the Room of the Last Supper are located within the remains of a Crusader basilica. The basilica in turn was built over a huge ruined fifth

Dormition tower and dome

century church known as Hagia Zion, Holy
Zion, named for Isaiah's words *"And the
law will come forth from Zion, and the
word of the Lord from Jerusalem"* (Isaiah
2:3).

Other Christian traditions are connected
to Mount Zion. On its slope, early
archaeological excavations revealed the
remains of a mansion believed to be the
House of Caiphas where Peter denied
Jesus, and where Jesus appeared before
the Sanhedrin. Over the site, a church and
monastery of the Assumptionist Fathers
stands, known as St. Peter in Gallicantu
(St. Peter at cock-crow).

Right: the crypt of the Dormition Church with a statue of Mary in eternal rest beneath a mosaic dome depicting Old Testament heroines. Below: the Dormition sanctuary

A Hebrew inscription indicating the burial place of Uzziah, King of Judah. The provenance of the inscription on what may have been Uzziah's tombstone is unknown. It is tempting to imagine that it was removed from the royal burial crypt where King David was also buried.

The cloth-covered cenotaph, or burial monument, that marks the Tomb of King David. Atop the monument are silver cases containing Torah scrolls (the Five Books of Moses) and Torah crowns (decorations placed atop Torah scrolls) donated to this sacred site by Jewish communities around the world.

Prayer books in the anteroom of King David's Tomb

Below: The Peter in Gallicantu Church. At left: an ancient flight of stairs leads up to the church and is believed to be those trod by Jesus on his way to trial at the House of Caiphas, the site commemorated by the church.

The mosaic-adorned interior of the Church of Peter in Gallicantu

Aerial view of Mount Zion's Dormition Abbey and King David's Tomb . At center left, the ancient reservoir now called the Sultan's Pool. Above it, the red-roofed houses of the nineteenth century neighborhood of Yemin Moshe and modern west Jerusalem.

Mount of Olives

Olive tree in the Garden of Gethsemane

The sanctity of the Mount of Olives harks back to the prophecy of Zechariah 14:4: "And his feet shall stand in that day on the mount of Olives, which is before Jerusalem on the east..." Jewish tradition came to understand this prophecy as a description of the End of Days, when the Messiah would arrive. As belief in the resurrection of the dead eventually established itself, Jews began to view burial on the Mount of Olives as a means of being among the first to witness the coming of the Messiah and the miracle of resurrection. To this day, the Jewish cemetery on the Mount of Olives functions as the largest Jewish cemetery in the world.

The Mount of Olives is also known as the Mount of Anointing. Kings of Judah were anointed here, and the olive oil for the ceremony was said to come from trees that grew on its slopes. In days gone by, a bonfire lit from the summit announced the commencement of Jewish festivals. During periods when Jews were not permitted to enter the Holy City the Mount of Olives, with its spectacular view of the Temple Mount, became a

meaningful venue for their prayers and lamentations. It has become a favorite starting point for generations of pilgrims beginning their Jerusalem experience.

During Second Temple times rabbis and sages, inspired by the sight of Judaism's holiest place, would preach to their disciples from its slopes. Jesus, too, chose this site for many of his most moving discourses about the Holy City. According to one tradition, Jesus taught the Lord's prayer here. And at this place, where David had wept for his rebellious

Interior of the Church of All Nations

Mosaic facade of the Church of All Nations

son Absalom (2 Sam 15:30), Jesus wept over the coming destruction of the Temple (Luke 19:37). On Palm Sunday, Jesus descended one of its paths astride a white donkey through a joyful crowd.

At the Garden of Gethsemane, at the foot of the Mount of Olives, John 18:2 says that "Jesus oftimes resorted thither with his disciples". Here he was betrayed by Judas and arrested. And in a link between Old Testament and New, the Mount of Olives is marked as the location of Jesus' return to earth (Acts 1:1-12).

Greek Orthodox service at the entrance to the Tomb of Mary

Steps descend to the crypt in the Crusader-era Tomb of Mary

The Dome of the Ascension on the Mount of Olives marks the place where Jesus ascended to heaven.

The traditional footprint of Jesus preserved within the Dome of the Ascension

The Russian Orthodox Church of Mary Magdalene was built on the Mount of Olives in 1885 by Czar Alexander III in memory of his mother Empress Maria.

Palm Sunday procession walks down the Mount of Olives in the footsteps of Jesus

Cloister of the Pater Noster Church, the site where Jesus is said to have taught the Lord's Prayer, adorned with the Pater Noster prayer in dozens of languages. The church was built on land purchased in the mid-nineteenth century by a French noblewoman.

Altar in the Dominus Flevit Chapel

Bethany

Mark and Luke both note that Bethany was located on the Mount of Olives, with John (John 11:18) adding the detail that it was fifteen stadia (or about two miles) from Jerusalem. It was here that Jesus raised Lazarus from the dead. Jesus knew the family of Lazarus—Lazarus' sister Martha had "received him into her house" and their sister Mary was one of Jesus' disciples (Luke 10:38-39).

Present-day Bethany is named in Arabic in honor of its most famous citizen; it is called El-azariyah, or the town of Lazarus.

Christian presence in the town begins in the third century. A tomb, which has figured prominently in pilgrims' diaries for centuries, is surrounded by churches past and present, as well as a mosque dedicated to Lazarus and constructed in the sixteenth century. The Roman Catholic Church of St. Lazarus, another accomplishment of Italian architect Antonio Barluzzi in the Holy Land, is adorned with insightful mosaics depicting the sacred stories which tradition says took place on this spot.

The churches and minaret over the traditional house of Lazarus, Mary and Martha in Bethany

68

The Kedron Valley

The Kedron Valley lies east of the Old City, between the Temple Mount and the Mount of Olives. The ancients envisioned the Messiah crossing the Kedron to enter Jerusalem, and so they accorded the valley spiritual significance: It came to be identified with the Valley of Jehoshaphat, where the Prophet Joel envisioned the scene of the Last Judgment (Joel 3:2). Medieval Christian pilgrim Felix Fabri describes a custom whereby pilgrims piled up stones in the Kedron Valley in order to mark the particular spot where they would stand on that day.

Jewish and Muslim legends relate that two bridges will miraculously span the Kedron Valley at the End of Days; a strong one will bear the righteous to the Temple Mount, while the wicked will attempt to cross a bridge of paper that will collapse under their weight.

View of the ancient Kedron Valley tombs from the new Mount of Olives promenade.

The Tomb of Absalom

Interior of the tomb of the sons of Hezir in the Kedron Valley

68

View of the Hebrew University, founded in 1925 on Mount Scopus

Mt. Scopus

The Augusta Victoria complex with its landmark tower is located between the Mount of Olives and Mount Scopus. Its cornerstone was laid in 1898 when German King Wilhelm II visited Jerusalem, naming it in honor of his wife. The structure was intended to house German pilgrims, but instead it served from 1920-1925 as the residence of the British High Commissioner. Later it became a hospital, now under the auspices of the Lutheran World Federation.

Notre Dame de France, built in 1887, was constructed as a pilgrims' hostel with funds donated by French Catholic philanthropist Baron de Pielat. This was a time of energetic construction by all of the European powers—they attempted to turn real estate gains into political power by purchasing tracts of land all over the city, including Jaffa Road (the Russians), Mount Zion and the Mount of Olives (the Germans) and Prophets' Street (the Italians). Todays European visitors can recognize in some of Jerusalem's nineteenth century buildings replicas of famous monuments in their own cities.

This statue, by American sculptor Alexander Leiberman, entitled "Faith", is located near Mount Scopus. Differing aspects of its interconnected geometric forms are revealed from different perspectives with a circular form placed to deduce that all other forms are linked to it.

The Hebrew University's amphitheater with the Judean Wilderness in the background

70

Tombs of the Kings, Second Temple-era burial cave of Queen Helene of Adiabe, a convert to Judaism who came with her family to live in the Holy City.

Anthropomorphic vase, Jericho, 18th-17th century BCE
Photography: Rockefeller Museum

The Rockefeller Museum

Built in the 1930's during the period of the British Mandate, the architecture of the Rockefeller Museum is reminiscent of that of the fine museums of Europe's capitals. Its spacious halls house an important collection of Land of Israel antiquities, a must for visiting archaeology buffs. During the Six-Day War the battle for Jerusalem raged around the museum. The Rockefeller Museum today is also home to the offices of the Israel Antiquities Authority, the Dead Sea Scrolls (now undergoing restoration), as well as a fine library of history and archeology.

Cup from Lachish, 14th-15th century BCE
photography: Rockefeller Museum

Antiquities on display in the Rockefeller Museum

The Garden Tomb

In 1883, General Charles Gordon visited Jerusalem. From the window of his lodgings in a house above the Damascus Gate, he spied a rocky outcropping to the north and was immediately impressed with its resemblance to a skull. Reminded of the New Testament description of the place of Jesus' execution as "a place called Golgotha, that is to say, a place of a skull"

Interior of the Garden Tomb

(Matt 27:33)—he concluded that this singular-looking rock must be the place of Crucifixion.

A rock-hewn tomb discovered in close proximity to the skull-shaped mound strengthened the identification, as did the presence of a large water

View of Skull Hill

cistern, a fixture in gardens or orchards of antiquity. Here then are all the visual elements of the place of Crucifixion and burial as described in the Gospel of John: "At the place where Jesus was crucified, there was a garden and in the garden a new tomb..." (John 19:41). Since 1894, the Garden Tomb has belonged to the non-denominational British-based Garden Tomb Association.

View of the Garden Tomb

Mishkenot She'ananim

Until 1860, when Moses Montefiore built his windmill and new neighborhood on the slope of the upper Hinnom Valley, not a soul lived outside the walls of Jerusalem. The gates of the city would clang shut at dusk and not reopen until sunrise. Anyone unlucky enough to be caught outside the city risked mortal danger at the hands of marauders, or even wild animals, according to one contemporary newspaper account!

But with the construction of the windmill together with a neighborhood which Montefiore optimistically named Mishkenot She'ananim, "peaceful habitations" (Isaiah 32:18), the "New City" was born. The project was funded with money left to the Jews of Jerusalem by American Jewish community leader Judah Touro of whose will Montefiore was executor.

The mill was to grind wheat and provide a livelihood for the residents of the new quarter. Oddly, despite state-of-the-art machinery imported from England, and for reasons still in controversy, the mill never turned a blade! During the years when Jerusalem was divided the windmill stood dilapidated and forlorn on what had become the border of the divided city. Only after the Six Day War was the area restored to become one of Jerusalem's most charming districts.

Moses Montefiore

Meah Shearim

Meah Shearim, founded in 1874, was one of the pioneering neighborhoods of the New City. The name, meaning "one hundred-fold" has double significance. First, the number of homes to be built by the group of families which founded the neighborhood was to be one hundred. Second, the

week that the neighborhood was founded, the Torah portion to be read included God's blessing to Isaac wherein his yield was increased "one hundred fold" (Gen 26:12).

Religious study is still the most salient aspect of the lives of the residents of Meah Shearim. It is one of the bastions of Judaism's Ultra-Orthodox stream, comprising dozens of groups which differ from one another regarding the particular rabbi or school of Orthodox practice they follow. One of the best known of these groups are the Hassidim, a sect founded in Poland in the eighteenth century. The Hassidic movement rejected the Jewish leadership of the day, which

they regarded as overly authoritarian, and initiated practices of ecstatic prayer, dancing, and reliance on charismatic leaders as equally legitimate paths to religious fulfillment. Eventually, despite the often vitriolic opposition of other sects, this movement gained the widespread popularity it enjoys today.

An astute observer will be able to note variations in attire that differentiate one group of ultra-Orthodox Jews from another. All, however, are extremely committed to their way of life to the exclusion of many aspects of the modern culture that prevail beyond the borders of their community.

Scenes in Meah Shearim

Downtown Jerusalem

Jaffa Road was the New City's first paved street. It received its name from the link it formed between Jerusalem and the ancient port of Jaffa. In the mid-nineteenth century, the Russian Orthodox Church purchased a choice piece of land on the north side of Jaffa road, where a pilgrim's hostel and church were constructed. Today, the church is a Jerusalem landmark.

At the eastern end of Jaffa Road Road facing the Old City walls the new Jerusalem municipality complex was opened in 1993. Its prize-winning design successfully preserves historical facades. Among other downtown landmarks are the Great Synagogue on King George Street. Further afield on King David Street are the impressive King David Hotel, constructed in 1931, and the beautiful old Jerusalem YMCA, whose architecture represents the various historical periods of the city.

Green swaths are not lacking even in Jerusalem's heart: Independence Park and Liberty Bell Garden are among center-city's favorite family gathering places.

Jaffa Road's Mahane Yehuda fruit and vegetable market

"Modern Head, 1975/90" by Roy Lichtenstein. In the background is the impressive new Jerusalem Municipality complex

The Russian Orthodox Church

The Sherover Theater introduces a modern accent to the capital's stately Talbiyeh quarter

The Ben Yehuda Pedestrian Mall

The triangle formed by center-city's Ben Yehuda, Jaffa, and King George Streets is the heart of Jerusalem's commercial district. It grew up during the British Mandate era, eclipsing the picturesque nearby nineteenth century neighborhood of Nahalat Shiv'a, which soon fell into disrepair. By the 1970's, a plan was afoot to raze Nahalat Shiv'a and rebuild the area with high-rise office buildings. Luckily, city planners changed their minds, and the charming old quarter was restored. Its restaurants, outdoor cafes, and boutiques, located along Solomon and Rivlin streets off of Zion Square and in shady adjacent stone courtyards combine to make it one of the city's most popular shopping districts for visitors and locals alike.

Preserved facade of the old Talitha Kumi Orphanage adorns King George Street

View of Zion Square

The new Jerusalem Municipality complex

The Israel Museum

The landmark Israel Museum is Israel's national home of archaeology, art, and Judaica. The unique white-peaked dome of the Shrine of the Book provides a place of honor for the exhibit of a small number of the Dead Sea Scrolls, the oldest Hebrew biblical writings in existence. Its distinctive design reminds visitors of the shape of the covers of the clay jars in which the original scrolls were found. The Museum's Youth Wing, a concept developed in Israel, contains challenging didactic exhibitions.

The Israel Museum is the country's largest. It was constructed in 1965 as one stage in the fulfillment of an ambitious city plan for the capital: This part of western Jerusalem was set aside to be a center for culture, education (the Hebrew University's Givat Ram campus, built to take the place of the old Hebrew University on Mount Scopus which had become inaccessible on the other side of the then-divided Jerusalem) and government, with the Knesset and government offices.

In recent years, the Biblelands Museum and the Science Museum have joined the Israel Museum in fulfilling the cultural aspect of the plan, and the magnificent new Supreme Court has also been built here. A green frame for this picture is ensured by the popular Sacher Park flanking the area on one side, with the age-old Monastery of the Cross and its surrounding olive groves, and the University's tranquil botanical gardens on the other.

Above: tiny inscribed ivory pomegranate, mid-eighth century BCE
Photography: Nahum Slepak

View of the Israel Musem at dusk

77

Hoshana, a page from an Italian prayerbook, fifteenth century
Photography: David Harris

Torah scroll case, Afghanistan

Bronze bust of Hadrian, 125-138 CE

Jan Victors, the Dismissal of Hagar

Spice boxes (18th-20th centuries) from the Israel Museum's Judaica collection. Photography: Nahum Slepak

A portion of the Isaiah Scroll

The Shrine of Book

Home of the Dead Sea Scrolls, the Israel Museum's Shrine of the Book is famous for the symbolism of ts design. Its peaked white dome is reminiscent of the covers of the tall clay jars in which the original scrolls --the oldest Hebrew Bible manuscripts ever discovered--were found by a Bedouin shepherd in a cave at Qumran in the Judean Wilderness in July of 1947. In stark contrast to the dome's gentle curves, a black wall stands behind it. The choice of colors hints at the scroll entitled "The War of the Children of Light Against the Children of Darkness" which embodies the beliefs of its writers about the End of Days. Within the Shrine, a central display case represents the wooden roller of a Torah scroll. The Shrine houses an exhibit about the beliefs and lifestyle of the Dead Sea Sect, "A Day at Qumran"

Interior of the Shrine of the Book

An inkwell discovered in the ruins of Qumran, the Essene settlement

American architects Keisler and Bartos' white dome and black wall are among Jerusalem's most distinctive landmarks.

Biblelands Museum Jerusalem

The outstanding antiquities on exhibit in the Biblelands Museum Jerusalem are rare treasures that tell the story of the cultural and spiritual life of the ancient peoples of the Bible lands Displays are accompanied by appropriate scriptural texts which help visitors visualize how the various objects were used in Bible times.

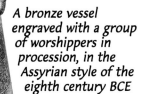

A bronze vessel engraved with a group of worshippers in procession, in the Assyrian style of the eighth century BCE

An ivory plaque typical of ninth-century BCE Phoenician style that may have resembled the cherubim in Solomon's Temple

The illuminated Knesset, as seen from the Israel Museum's Shrine of the Book

The Knesset

Israel's parliament is named for the Jewish governing body of the early Second Temple Period, and means "assembly". The number of its members, 120, is identical to the number of members of that ancient body. The Knesset moved to Jerusalem from its first home in Tel Aviv in 1949. For nearly two decades thereafter, Israel's legislators met in a building on the capital's King George Street. Finally, in 1966, the Knesset moved "home" to its present complex.

The Declaration of Independence

The Knesset's Chagall Hall

Bronze Menorah, gift of Great Britain, in the plaza opposite the Knesset

The Supreme Court

Within sight of the Knesset rises the imposing Supreme Court building. Designed by the brother-sister team of Ram Karmi and Ada Karmi-Melamed, the Supreme Court was completed in 1992, Israel's last government institution to find a permanent home. Both biblical themes and contemporary life influenced the architects in their masterful choice of motifs. A graceful stone entrance corridor reminiscent of a Jerusalem alleyway leads to the library roofed by a pyramid— inspired by Absalom's Tomb— that rises above the library and through which sunshine floods the area, symbolic of the enlightenment of justice.

Hall opposite the courtrooms, lit only by natural light

View of the Supreme Court complex

Yad Vashem

The name of Israel's Holocaust Commemoration Authority, Yad Vashem, means "everlasting name" and comes from Isaiah 56:5, "I will give them an everlasting name, that will not be cut off". The mandate of Yad Vashem, stipulated by law, is to perpetuate the memory of the six million victims of the Holocaust perpetrated by the Nazis on the Jews of Europe during World War II.

Yad Vashem maintains the largest archive in the world of Holocaust-related material, containing over 50 million pages of documents, with a library housing over 72,000 titles and thousands of periodicals. An international school of Holocaust studies offers educational activities to children and adults from around the world. Yad Vashem seeks out non-Jews, known as Righteous Gentiles, to honor them for risking their lives to

"The Silent Cry" stands outside the Hall of Remembrance

aid and protect Jewish victims. Yad Vashem also maintains an archive containing the names of millions of victims. The forty-five acre site contains a Historical Museum, Children's Memorial, a Central Commemoration Hall and the Valley of the Communities, a dramatic monument dug from bedrock.

Statue depicting educator Janusz Korzak accompanying his young charges to their deaths

The Valley of the Communities

Mt. Herzl

Section of the Military Cemetery

In 1950, the remains of the founder of Zionism, Theodor Herzl, were brought from Vienna to be reinterred on the mountain that now bears his name. Herzl, who died in 1904, lobbied tirelessly to turn an ancient biblical idea—the return of the Jewish people to their ancestral homeland—into the modern political movement that resulted in the founding of the State of Israel. Israel's national military cemetery is also situated on Mount Herzl.

Tomb of Yitzhak Rabin

Tomb of Theodor Herzl

Hadassah Hospital

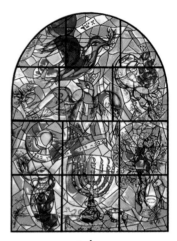

Benjamin   *Judah*   *Asher*

The first home of Hadassah hospital was on Mount Scopus where it was built in the early years of the British Mandate. From 1947-1967, when the rest of Jerusalem was cut off from Mount Scopus, the hospital was forced to close its doors. To replace it, the founders, the Hadassah Women's Organization, constructed a new facility on the western side of town overlooking the biblical hamlet of Ein Karem.

As the hospital neared completion, the time came to find a unique and significant decor for its synagogue. World-famous Russian Jewish artist Marc Chagall was called upon for the task. The last chapter of Genesis, in which Jacob blesses his sons, was Chagall's inspiration for the design he donated to Hadassah. Each of the twelve stained-glass windows he created is rich in symbolism taken from the stories of the relationships between the twelve brothers. The extraordinary depth of color and three-dimensional effects, as well as the use of abstract forms to depict complex yet comprehensible themes, have made the Chagall windows one of the great works of art of the twentieth century.

The Chagall Synagogue's interior is illuminated like a jewel at night

The Model of Ancient Jerusalem
at the Time of the Second Temple
in the Grounds of the Holyland Hotel Jerusalem

General view of the city, looking west. In the foreground: the Temple Mount

Herod's Theater

The tomb of David

The Hasmonean palace

The Palace of the High Priest Caiaphas

Upper City mansions

Ein Karem

Scenic Ein Karem is typical of the villages around Jerusalem. The region's numerous vineyards, some of them astride ancient terraces, gave this village its name, which means "spring of the vineyard." They are reminiscent of the biblical blessing to Judah, whose descendants lived in this area: "Judah washed his garments in wine" (Genesis 49:11) has long been regarded as "in the hill country...into a city of Juda" (Luke 1:39) that was the home of Elizabeth and Zachariah, the parents of John the Baptist.

Within the village are two churches marking the events

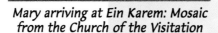

recorded in Luke. One, the seventeenth-century Church of St. John the Baptist, was erected by the Crusaders over the remains of a fifth century church marking John's birth place. The second, the Church of the Visitation, is on a slope overlooking the village. The courtyard of the Church of the Visitation is adorned with plaques with the words of the Magnificat in numerous languages. The spring, known as the Fount of the Virgin, still courses gently out of the mountainside in the center of town.

Mary arriving at Ein Karem: Mosaic from the Church of the Visitation

View of Ein Karem, with the Church of John the Baptist at the center

Left: the well in the Church of the Visitation where Mary met Elizabeth. Above the well, murals of Mary and Elizabeth's meeting and the Murder of the Innocents, from which John was miraculously hidden. Below: the courtyard of the Church of the Visitation.

Left: Marble relief depicting the baptism of Jesus by John. Right: Grotto of the birth of John in the Church of St. John. Below: View of the Church of St. John the Baptist.

Bethlehem

"*But* thou, Bethlehem, Ephrata, though thou be little among the thousands of Judah, yet out of thee shall he come forth that is to be ruler in Israel..."(Micah 5:2).

Grotto of the Nativity

Birthplace of Jesus in the Grotto of the Nativity

Bethlehem

In this passage, Micah alludes to the future birth of the Messiah in Bethlehem, and the savior's kinship to David, also born there.

Bethlehem is indeed a small town when compared with its near neighbor, Jerusalem. Nonetheless, . great events knocked at its gates. David's nephew and chief-of-staff Joab was born here. Samuel anointed David king in Bethlehem. And during the tempestuous days of the Philistine-Israelite conflict, while the city was under Philistine siege, David's loyal band of mighty men sneaked into town to get water for the king.

When the decree of Caesar Augustus ordered all Jews to be counted, the New Testament relates that Joseph and Mary, of the tribe of Judah and the line of David, came to their ancestral home for the census. Mary was in an advanced stage of pregnancy, and so it was

Crusader paintings on the Byzantine columns in the Church of the Nativity comprise one of the largest collections of medieval wall paintings in the world.

Interior of the Greek Orthodox Basilica of the Nativity

Manger Square and the Church of the Nativity

90

Olive wood carving is one of Bethlehem's most ancient crafts.

that in Bethlehem the event occurred that made the town famous forever: the birth of Jesus.

It is an irony of history that pagan shrines may have served to mark the holy spots, instead of wiping out their memory as they were presumably intended to do. For in the fourth century, when church-building did commence, one of the first churches constructed was the Church of the Nativity on the very site where the Romans had put up a shrine to Adonis.

Momentous events of Christian history are linked to Bethlehem. Here St. Jerome penned the Vulgate, his translation of the Bible from Hebrew into Latin. The Crusading army came to Bethlehem in 1099, even before they conquered Jerusalem; later, King Baldwin I was crowned here. The Church of the Nativity remains the core of an energetic local Christian community as well as a magnet for pilgrims from around the world.

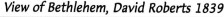

Bethlehem market scenes

View of Bethlehem, David Roberts 1839

The Flight to Egypt, detail from the Milk Grotto Church

Facade of the Milk Grotto Church, where tradition says Mary nursed the baby Jesus

Interior of St.Catherine's Church, yearly venue for Bethlehem's Catholic Midnight Mass

The procession marking the arrival of the Roman Catholic Patriarch from Jerusalem on Christmas eve.

The Magi (Matthew 2:1-11) may have arrived from the east by camel caravan to lay their treasures before the baby Jesus.

Shepherds' Fields

Just east of Bethlehem, facing the rolling hills of the Judean wilderness, a strip of arable land separates the settled highlands from the desert. Here, from time immemorial, wheat and barley have been raised. Significantly, the town east of Bethlehem is known as Beit Sahour, or "House of Stone" hinting at the inhospitable desert beyond.

Painting of the Nativity in the Chapel of Shepherds' Fields

The wheat and barley fields are known as the "fields of Boaz" The Book of Ruth relates that Ruth, the great-great-grandmother of King David and ancestress of Jesus, after her arrival from Moab in the company of her mother-in-law Naomi, a native of Bethlehem, worked in these fields and later married their owner, Boaz.

All travelers arriving from the wilderness would pass through these fields on their way to Bethlehem. Thus it was that the shepherds, whose pasture lands lay in the wilderness to the east, were *"keeping watch over their flocks at night"* (Luke 2:8) when an angel of the Lord appeared to them and said *"Fear not: for behold, I bring you good tidings of great joy, which shall be to all people"* (Luke 2:10). And the shepherds said to one another *"Let us now go even unto Bethlehem, and see this thing which is come to pass, which the Lord has made known unto us"* (Luke 2:15).

The Chapel of Shepherds' Fields, with its distinctive slanted walls, is reminiscent of the tents in which the shepherds may have dwelt.

Bethlehem from the east, where shepherds pasture their flocks as in ancient times

Rachel's Tomb

Rachel the matriarch died unexpectedly near Bethlehem after giving birth to Benjamin, the youngest of the twelve sons of Jacob. Jacob was unable to bury her in the family tomb at Hebron, so he interred her *"in the way to Efrata which is Bethlehem"* (Genesis 35:19). *"And Jacob set up a pillar upon her grave"*, relates Genesis, *"that is the pillar of Rachel's grave to this day"* (Genesis 35: 19-20). The pillar is long gone, but the grave of Rachel is still revered on the selfsame road to Bethlehem.

The poignant story of Rachel, beloved of Jacob's wives and childless until she finally conceived Joseph, has made her one of the Bible's most beloved characters. Childless women feel especially close to this matriarch and pilgrimage to the tomb to offer prayer is considered auspicious in such straits.

Echoes of Rachel's story appear elsewhere in the Bible. Jeremiah, when lamenting the exile of Judah's inhabitants in the wake of the Babylonian destruction, uttered the immortal words: *"A voice was heard in Ramah, a voice of lamentation and bitter weeping. Rachel weeping for her children, refused to be comforted for her children, because they were not"* (Jeremiah 31: 15). Matthew, aware of the proximity of Rachel's tomb to Bethlehem, quotes this passage when relating the tale of the murder of the innocent children by Herod the Great after the birth of Jesus (Matthew 2:18).

The velvet cover over the Tomb of Rachel is inscribed with the words of Jeremiah 31:15

View of Herodion, east of Bethlehem. Here, on the site of one of Herod the Great's early military victories, he constructed an artificial hill capped by a luxurious fortress-palace. Historian Josephus Flavius records that Herod's body was brought from Jericho for burial here, although archaeologists have as yet found no trace of the tomb.

Hebron

Hebron, home of the Tomb of the Patriarchs, and the city from which David first ruled, is one of Judaism's most significant locales. Together with Jerusalem, Safed, and Tiberias, Hebron is counted among the four holy cities of the land of Israel.

An immense complex built by Herod the Great today marks the Tomb of the Patriarchs in Hebron. It stands over the Cave of Machpela which Abraham purchased to serve as a family tomb. No better example exists of Middle Eastern negotiations than this story, related in Genesis 23, in which the owner of the property, Ephron the Hittite, full of fine words, entices Abraham to pay much more for the land than the Patriarch had originally intended!

The Tomb of the Patriarchs is the burial place of Abraham, Isaac and Jacob, Sarah, Rebecca and Lea, and, according to ancient legends, both Joseph and Esau. Jewish tradition sees this site also as the burial place of Adam and Eve. The excellent state of preservation of the ancient compound is a sign of the singular importance attached to it by all inhabitants of the Holy Land throughout the ages. The tombs are said to be located

Aerial view of Hebron, with the Tomb of Machpela in the foreground

within caves beneath the floor of the building, the interior of which dates mainly from the Crusader period. Tradition forbids entry into the caves and indeed, very few have seen them with their own eyes. The faithful recite their prayers in front of small hipped-roofed structures in which cenotaphs mark the site of the tombs below.

Steps leading up to the Tomb of the Patriarchs. The walls date from the period of Herod the Great.

This small structure houses the cenotaph marking the tomb of Isaac

Mamre

The Plain of Mamre is first mentioned as the dwelling place of Abraham in Genesis 14:13. Here, In the shade of its ancient oak trees Abraham greeted the angels that informed him of the birth of Isaac, as he "...sat in the tent door in the heat of the day. And he lifted up his eyes and looked, and lo, three men stood by him, and when he saw them, he ran to meet them" (Genesis 18:1-2). During the Roman era Mamre became the site of market fairs and yearly festivals, with a decidedly pagan flavor about them, which ended with the advent of Christianity in the fourth century. Excavations at Mamre have unearthed Herodian, and Hadrianic structures, as well as a massive church dating to the time of Emperor Constantine.

The famous "Hebron glass" is still hand-blown in the ancient city

Massive ancient walls at Mamre

The Judean Lowlands

Perhaps in a larger country, the band of rolling hills known as the Judean lowlands would go unnoticed. Not so in the Holy Land, where every inch of territory has significance, geographical, strategic, spiritual, and most often a combination of all three! The lowlands are passageway or barrier, as the case may be, between the flatlands of the Coastal Plain in the west and the high mountains of Judea in the east. Any army which sought to approach Judea from the coast would have to pass through the lowlands. On the other hand, any fighting force ensconced along its winding river valleys or hidden in its numerous caves could hold off even the best-equipped enemy.

This is a land of many heroes: In one of its approaches, the Elah Valley, David fought Goliath; Samson was born here, between the towns of Tzor'a and Eshta'ol, not far from Beit Shemesh, beyond which Philistine country stretched to the sea. Rehoboam fortified its cities. And the rag-tag forces of Judah the Maccabee kept the well-trained Seleucid army at bay here, their heavy weapons and tight formations a burden in the hilly region the Maccabean locals knew so intimately.

Today the lowlands of Judah are coming into their own. Archaeologists are busy unearthing the rich history of the region, now viewed and appreciated by legions of visitors.

A magnificent limestone cave at the Avshalom Reserve near the Ayalon Valley, above the town of Beit Shemesh

View of the Elah Valley looking west towards the Judean Hills

Beit Govrin

Beit Govrin is first mentioned by Josephus Flavius in his Wars of the Jews, as a Jewish village that fell to Roman general Vespasian in 68. At the end of the Great Revolt, the village became a densely inhabited Jewish city, which became a center of the Bar Kokhba uprising 64 years later. The region surrounding Beit Govrin is endowed with a unique geological attribute: a thin layer of hard limestone overlays soft, easy-to-quarry chalk. The ancients merely had to perforate the hard limestone and burrow downward in a circular, ever-widening pattern. In so doing, they were able to dig out bell-shaped basement storage areas,

The Apolonius cave, a richly adorned burial cavern of a wealthy hellenistic family of Beit Govrin

water cisterns, dovecotes, rooms in which to manufacture olive oil, tombs, and hideouts for the revolutionaries against Rome. The chalk itself was touted far and wide as an excellent building material.

A tell rising above the landscape is ancient Mareisha, already an important city in the Israelite period. Many of the most interesting grottos once served as basements of houses of the Hellenistic town Marissa, that eventually occupied the slopes of the tell.

Remains of a Crusader church on Byzantine foundations

Colombarium cave where doves were raised in Hellenistic times

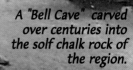

A "Bell Cave" carved over centuries into the solf chalk rock of the region.

98

Emmaus

It was on the road to this lowlands village that Jesus appeared to the disciples after the Resurrection (Luke 24:13-35). Two other locales have been identified as Emmaus over the centuries, but the remains of a Byzantine basilica here, as well as the preservation of the ancient name in the name of the adjacent Arab village, Amwas, bode well for the accurate identification of this site with the Emmaus of the New Testament.

Facade of the nineteenth-century church at the Judean hills site of Emmaus

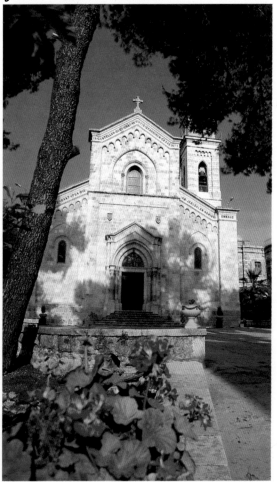

The Church of Notre Dame de l'Arche d'Alliance ("Our Lady of the Ark of the Covenant") in biblical Kiryat Yearim overlooks Abu Ghosh, a town considered by some traditions to be New Testament Emmaus.

Remains of a Byzantine Church at Emmaus in the Ayalon Valley

Inn of the Good Samaritan

On the Way to Jericho

The Christian monastic movement began when spiritually committed individuals withdrew from society to lead lives of prayer and contemplation in the wilderness. This they did in imitation of biblical characters such as Elijah, Jesus and John the Baptist, all of whom sought the strictures of the desert for spiritual inspiration.

Eventually, individual monks were joined by others who had heard of their great spiritual powers. Communities coalesced, some numbering many hundreds at their zenith. In some monasteries, called lauras, monks lived a solitary life, each in his own cell or cave, meeting the others only for prayers. Other monasteries were more communal, their inhabitants working at basket and mat weaving and rope-making, in addition to the raising of food. Some monasteries served pilgrims, maintaining special areas for lodgings and medical care.

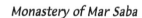

Monasteries in the Holy Land were often located close to sites associated with biblical events. They flourished until the Persian conquest of 614 CE put an end to many of them. The Muslim conquest later in the century led to even greater decline, and very few have survived into the modern age.

St. George's Monastery, founded by John of Thebes, later known as John of Chosiba, is an example of a coenobium, or a communal monastery, although some of its members follow the anchorite tradition and live in caves some distance from the central complex. The monastery, restored in the nineteenth century, is located in Wadi Kelt, the magnificent canyon through which the ancient Jerusalem-Jericho road once passed.

Monastery of Mar Saba

Restored mosaics at the Martyrios Monastery in Ma'ale Adumim

St. George's Monastery, Wadi Kelt

Jericho, surrounded by date palms, in the sixth-century mosaic Madaba Map

Jericho

At Jericho, the first walled city in the world was constructed some ten thousand years ago. Jericho's earliest fortifications are still visible, in the form of a massive, skillfully-constructed tower. Archaeologists have excavated Jericho extensively in the search for the famous walls conquered by Joshua, but the results have been disappointing: Most archaeologists concede that no fortifications have been identified from the presumed time of Joshua's entrance into the Holy Land, a fact which has provided fascinating grist for the historians' mills over the years.

Still, standing atop the ancient mound,

Hisham's Palace, a luxurious villa constructed by the Ommayads in the eighth century

The sycomore tree believed to be the one Zacchaeus the tax collector climbed to get a better view of Jesus (Luke 19:4)

The renowned fruit of Jericho for sale in the market

Numerous mountain springs enrich the soil of Jericho reaching it by way of aqueducts, both ancient and modern.

Tel Jericho's round neolithic tower (seen within the archaeological trench) dating to about 7000 BCE is part of the earliest city walls ever built.

it is easy to imagine the many biblical stories that took place in its environs. Jericho, called "the City of Palms" (Judges 1:16) became the backdrop for many an exciting tale in the years after the fateful day when trumpet blasts and the shouts of the Israelite army brought the ramparts crashing down (Joshua 6).

According to Joshua's edict, "cursed be the man before the Lord that riseth up and buildeth this city, Jericho" (Joshua 6:26). The Bible states that Joshua's curse came

Detail from the mosaic floor of Jericho's sixth century synagogue reads "peace on Israel"

true: "In [Ahab's] days did Hiel the Bethelite build Jericho: he laid the foundations thereof in Abiram his firstborn, and set up the gates thereof in his youngest son, Segub..." (1 Kings 16:34).

It was from Jericho that Elijah set out, in the company of his disciple and successor Elisha, to cross the River Jordan and be taken up into heaven in a fiery chariot. Elisha then "healed" Jericho's spring water by throwing salt into it, restoring the region's famed productivity after a period of agricultural disaster.

Byzantine bronze censer found at Jericho. Studium Biblicum Fransciscanum

According to tradition, on the barren cliffs overlooking the fertile orchards of Jericho, Jesus fasted for forty days and was tempted by the devil. On the road to Jericho, he healed a blind beggar, called Bartemaus (Mark 10:46) who then joined the triumphal procession of the faithful to Jerusalem.

Zacchaeus, a tax collector and a wealthy man clambered up into a sycomore tree to better get a glimpse of Jesus as he passed through town. This is not the unusual act it might appear to be at first; sycomore trees of the fig family abound in Jericho and other oases and during the summer season, as their fruit ripened, it was common to see farmers and their families in the trees cultivating the fruit.

Pilgrims' procession to the traditional site of baptism on the banks of the Jordan, near Kasr el-Yahud Monastery.

View of the Monastery of Temptation, where Jesus fasted and was tempted by the devil (Matt 4:1)

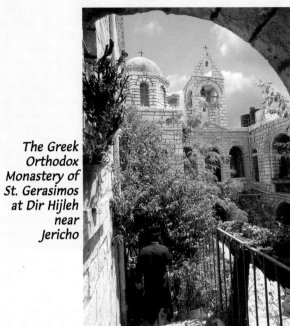

The Greek Orthodox Monastery of St. Gerasimos at Dir Hijleh near Jericho

Shrine at the baptismal site near the Jordan River

Pilgrims visit the traditional site of Jesus' baptism by John on the banks of the River Jordan east of Jericho.

The Dead Sea

The World's Lowest Lake

The name "Dead Sea" is never used to describe this body of water in the Bible, where it is known variously as "The Salt Sea" (Gen 14:3, Joshua 15:2), the Eastern Sea (Joel 2:20), The Sea of Arabah (2 Kings: 14:25), or simply "the sea" (Ezekiel 47:8).

Adventure tourism—a Dead Sea pastime

The Romans called it the Asphalt Sea, named for one of the compounds that congeals from the minerals within the water and floats up to the surface from time to time. The term "Dead Sea" began to be used around the Roman era, on the assumption that because of its great salt content (over 30%) no living thing could survive. That assumption held true until recently when scientists identified an algae thriving in its waters. This algae is a significant source of beta caroten, and is now being produced commercially.

This fascinating inland lake—the lowest in the world-is 45 miles long and about 10 miles wide. It owes its salinity to the mineral springs on its banks, as well as to yearly floods that rush down the numerous canyons around its banks after rainfall in the mountains over 1200 meters above. The flood water dissolves minerals in the limestone rocks, bringing them down to the lake where they remain suspended. During the long, torrid Holy Land summer, enormous amounts of water evaporate from the Dead Sea, leaving behind the minerals in greater proportions and giving the water its famed salty density.

Today, the Dead Sea is actually two separate lakes. The northern lake is some 2000 feet deep, whereas the southern segment has become a shallow reservoir, artificially maintained by a channel from the northern lake. Here are located the

Floating in the Dead Sea's buoyant waters is a must for every visitor.

hotels and spas where visitors bask in the sun and enjoy the curative powers of the water, especially for diseases of the skin. The southern reaches of the Dead Sea are also home to the Dead Sea Works, which extracts various minerals from the waters, mainly potash, which is used in fertilizer, and most recently, magnesium, for metal production. This body of water, shared by Israel on the west and the Hashemite Kingdom of Jordan on the east, is the region's most valuable natural resource.

"Lot's Wife", a salt formation at Mount Sodom overlooking the Dead Sea

Salt pillars on the shores of the Dead Sea

Some of the famous Dead Sea resort hotels

A fragment of the Habbakuk Commentary, housed in the Shrine of the Book in Jerusalem

Qumran

Qumran was home to the group of ascetics who, over two thousand years ago, wrote the Dead Sea Scrolls—the oldest extant Hebrew texts of the Bible. In sectarian writings discovered among the scrolls, the group calls itself *hayahad* — the community—but most scholars believe them to be the Essenes, a Jewish sect that existed during the Roman period. Of the Essenes Josephus writes, "These men are despised of riches; among them all there is no appearance of poverty or excess of riches, but everyone's possessions are intermingled with every other's possessions...When they have clothed themselves in white veils, they bathe their bodies in cold water...And as for their piety towards God, it is very extraordinary...Moreover [members] swear to preserve the books belonging to the sect."

A lively debate continues to swirl around the identity of the writers of the Dead Sea Scrolls, since the discovery of the first scrolls by a Bedouin shepherd a half-century ago. But in addition to the scrolls themselves, ample archaeological evidence exists of a devotion to water purification and a simple, communal lifestyle, all of which link the site to the Essenes.

A view of the marl plateau and Cave Four, where the largest cache of Dead Sea Scrolls was discovered

The largest cache of Dead Sea Scrolls was discovered by chance during excavations of the ruins in a marl cave some distance from the central complex. Whether this cavern was the sect's library, or the hiding place for their most treasured possessions, their scrolls, may well remain a mystery.

A clay jar in which the first Dead Sea Scrolls were discovered

One of the all-important water cisterns at Qumran

Scroll fragment and inkwell

View of the Qumran complex

The interior of Cave Four

Ein Gedi

Ein Gedi is a superb example of the miracle wrought by a "river in the wilderness." Amidst the craggy and forbidding landscape around it, the cool green shadows and sparkling waters of the Ein Gedi spring are a haven for all creatures. The power of nature is visible here: huge boulders are poised in canyon crevices, to which they tumbled in long-ago floods. Giant blocks of stone partially detached from the canyon walls during earthquakes are another exciting element of the scenery.

The rock walls of the Ein Gedi canyon contain many caves. Perhaps it was in one of these that David, escaping the wrath of King Saul, sought shelter. The Bible (I Samuel 24) relates that at Ein Gedi Saul finally let go his rage against his young former protégé, who had become the darling of the people, and the two reconciled their differences.

Ibex, or mountain goats, roam the Ein Gedi Reserve

Spotted leopards, once numerous, are all but extinct in the area.

A hyrax, the biblical coney (Prov. 30:26, Ps. 104:18)

Visitors enjoy one of the pools at the Ein Gedi Falls

Ein Gedi was a prosperous town in the Roman era, as attested to by this synagogue mosaic floor. Its residents were expert in the production of cosmetics from balsam, a plant worth its weight in gold.

hike up the Ein Gedi cliffs fords a dazzling vantage point

The Shulamith Falls in the Ein Gedi Reserve

Masada

Towering rock walls deter approach to this 400 meter-high plateau on three sides, and a nearly impossible climb awaits potential attackers on the fourth. These strategic advantages mandated the choice of Masada as a hideout by the Holy Land's first century BCE rulers, the Hasmoneans. But it was Herod the Great who turned this barren mountaintop into a unique fortified palace, to serve him under conditions of mortal danger, yet lacking no amenity or luxury. The remains of his lavish residences, ornate bathhouses, numerous storehouses and servants' quarters, as well as huge water cisterns, have been well-preserved in the dry conditions that prevail here.

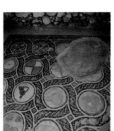

Detail of the mosaic in Masada's Byzantine church

About a century after Herod died, a small band of Jewish revolutionaries known as the Sicarii (and sometimes called the Zealots) took over the fortress as a base of operations against the Roman army. Roman-Jewish historian, Josephus Flavius, turned the spotlight onto the moving events that occurred there in his book "The Wars of the Jews".

Some three years after the destruction of the Templein 70 , the Roman Tenth Legion at last focused their attention on the Sicarii at Masada, the last pocket of resistance at the end of the Great Revolt. In a short time, they completed elaborate siege works, including eight sentry camps and a huge earthen ramp. Then they rolled their siege machines up the ramp and began the destruction of the perimeter wall of the fortress. Despite last-ditch attempts by the Jewish defenders to rebuild an inner wall that would withstand the blows of the Roman battering-rams, and a miraculous wind that Josephus says blew the Romans' blazing arrows back at them, the attack proceeded inexorably towards its conclusion.

Josephus relates that hours before the Romans broke into the fortress, Masada's leaders chose death for themselves and their families over surrender to the furious conqueror. Each father put his own wife and children to death with his sword, "feeling it to be the lightest of

Fluted columns and stucco adorned the walls of the peristyle.

View of Herod's palace

The peristyle, or colonnaded courtyard, on the lowest level of Herod's northern palace

evils", compared with the fate they feared for their loved ones if taken alive. Lots were drawn to choose ten men to kill all the other men, one to kill the other nine, and last of all himself.

Nineteen centuries later, Jews returned to the Holy Land. Searching for inspiration to spur themselves on to their nation-building goals, in 1963, archaeologists excavated Masada, first identified by nineteenth century explorers. Their discoveries highlighted Josephus' dramatic account of the resistance of the few against the many, and the tale took its place as one of the most emotionally powerful sagas of Jewish history.

Western entrance to Masada, near the point where Roman seige machines breached the wall.

The storerooms at Masada

The steam room of the bathhouse.

The plateau of Masada stands a thousand feet above the shores of the Dead Sea.

View of the northern section of Masada with Herod's palace

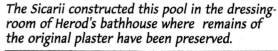

The Sicarii constructed this pool in the dressing-room of Herod's bathhouse where remains of the original plaster have been preserved.

Apse of Masada's Byzanitne church

Artist's rendering of the Masada fortress with the Roman ramp at right

Josephus Flavius

Josephus Flavius, chronicler of the dramatic events of the Second Temple era, and the only ancient source of information about Masada, was born in Jerusalem around 38 CE into a family of priests. At the age of 26, he made his first trip to Rome on a mission to secure the release of priests that had been imprisoned by Roman procurator Felix.

When the Great Revolt broke out in 66, Josephus became commander of the Galilee. But the cities he fortified fell one by one to the Romans. The last to fall, in 67 CE, was Jotapata, with Josephus himself in command. The last forty defenders—Josephus among them—fled to a cave and agreed upon a suicide pact. When only Josephus and one other man were left after the drawing of lots, Josephus persuaded the man to surrender with him to the Romans.

Earning the trust of the Roman general Vespasian, Josephus was released from captivity when the latter became emperor. Josephus eventually settled in Rome where he was granted citizenship and lived in the emperor's palace. Here he penned his best-known works, *The Jewish Wars*, and *The Antiquities of the Jews*. Because of Josephus' own participation in the events he chronicles, his works, though illuminating, have been the source of on-going debate as to the veracity of many details.

The chimney-like interior of a Mount Sodom salt cave

Mount Sodom

Mount Sodom is a virtually unique geological formation. It is composed of salt that congealed from Dead Sea water in an earlier age, eventually becoming overlaid with rock. When the rocky "envelope" cracked under the pressures of the area's frequent earth movements, the more pliable salt forced its way up through the fissures. Rain, even the scant two inches per year that falls here, wears away the rocky outer layers of Mount Sodom, but the salt is constantly pushed up from below.

Places where the salt protrudes or the rocky cap is particularly resistant to erosion have become a veritable "sculpture garden" of animal and human forms. It is not difficult to imagine Lot's Wife among them, turned into a pillar of salt as she looked back for the last time at the sinful city of Sodom before it dissolved in a hail of fire and brimstone.

The Salt Sea has bestowed upon Israel its most important natural resource: potash is one of the minerals drawn from its waters and made into fertilizer. A factory has recently opened for the production of magnesium, another one of the Dead Sea's treasures, an element that can be converted into a much sought-after lightweight, strong metal.

On the path to a salt cave at Mount Sodom

The Coastal Plain

*I*srael's coastal plain, bordering on the eastern shore of the Mediterranean Sea, is blessed with some of the country's largest streams as well as significant groundwater sources and fertile farmland.

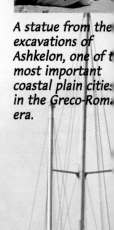

A statue from the excavations of Ashkelon, one of t most important coastal plain citie: in the Greco-Rom. era.

Throughout history, the coastal plain was inhabited by major players on the biblical stage: the Philistines in the south in the towns of Gaza, Ashkelon, Gath, Ashdod and Ekron, and the Phoenicians in the north in such towns as Dor and Acre.

Although Jews and Gentiles lived side-by-side in most of the cities of the coastal plain ,the character of the region remained primarily non-Jewish for most of its history. During the ascendancy of Christianity many coastal plain cities rose in importance. But as the Land of Israel lapsed into the lethargy of later times much of the good coastal soil, the "splendor" referred to in Isaiah 35:1, reverted to swamp and lay forsaken.

Only during the last century, with the draining of the swamps, has the coastal plain returned to take the significant place in the country that it held in days gone by. Today the coastal plain, between the modern port city of Ashdod in the south and the resort town of Netanya in the north, is Israel's most populous and developed region, and in fact one of the most crowded areas in the world.

...urch of St. Joseph of ...amathea in Ramleh

Detail of a large Roman-era mosaic recently unearthed in Lydda

Lydda

Lydda hosted a Christian community from the earliest days of the faith. Acts 9:32-35 relates, "As Peter passed through all quarters, he came down also to visit the saints which dwelt at Lydda. And there he found a certain man named Aeneas, which had kept his bed eight years, and was sick of the palsy. And Peter said unto him 'Aeneas, Jesus Christ maketh thee whole: arise, and make thy bed.' And he rose immediately. And all that dwelt in Lydda and Sharon saw him and turned to the Lord."

According to tradition, St. George the Dragon Slayer was a Lydda-born Roman soldier who accepted Christianity. Stories of his chivalrous acts became popular in England during the Crusades, eventually leading to his being named Patron Saint of that country.

St. George the Dragon-Slayer at Lydda's Greek Orthodox monsatery

View of the Greek Orthodox Church of St. George, Lydda

Ramleh

In the seventh century, the Muslims built a new city near the old Christian town of Lydda. During the ninth and tenth centuries, a lively Jewish community existed side by side with a Muslim majority, along with Karaites, a sect of Jewish origin that still maintains a synagogue in the town, and Samaritans. Fifteenth century Muslim historian Mujir a-Din borrowed from contemporary Jewish sources to report that Ramleh was the Philistine city of Gath, from where Goliath hailed. Yet another tradition notes that Ramleh was the home of Jonah the Prophet.

The tower of Ramleh's White Mosque, built in 716 and completed by Hisham (723-724) ,who also built the palace in Jericho that bears his name.

Jaffa

It was in Jaffa that Peter raised Tabitha from the dead, and later, from the rooftop of Simon the Tanner, he received the celestial call that preceded his trip to Caesarea and his conversion of Cornelius the Centurion.

By the time Jaffa first appears in the Bible, as part of the allotment of the tribe of Dan, it was already a city thousands of years old. As a port, it served every master of the land. Eventually, King Solomon established his own harbor here through which he imported the cedars of Lebanon to build the Temple. It was from the port of Jaffa that Jonah the prophet set sail for Tarshish. Jaffa's port, like all the other safe-havens on the Mediterranean coastline of the Holy Land, was eclipsed when Herod the Great constructed his world-famous harbor at Caesarea.

Even during the years of the Holy Land's decline, the port of Jaffa always knew the presence of European visitors and settlers, in some periods a substantial number. Napoleon's pestilence-ridden troops were quartered here after their retreat from the failed bid to take Acre in 1799. St. Peter's church, which must have been visible miles out to sea and a welcome sight for weary travelers, was founded by the Franciscans in 1854.

The fishing port of Jaffa

Jaffa's domes and spires were the first view of land spied by many a Holy Land Pilgrim

Jaffa illuminated on a festive summer evening

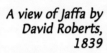

A view of Jaffa by David Roberts, 1839

Jaffa with the Church of St. Peter in the center, flanked by the city's park and the old port

Ramat Aviv Mall

Azrieli Center

Golda Center for the Performing Arts

Tel Aviv

Tel Aviv was founded at the turn of the century by Jewish pioneers, adjacent to the crumbling houses of its somnolent older sister, Jaffa. Seeking to transplant the latest European ideas of urban development to the shores of the Mediterranean, Tel Aviv's early days were marked by the construction of wide, tree-lined boulevards, and ceramic-adorned residences. Uncompromisingly modern, Tel Aviv is the epitome of fast-paced Israeli living, with a lively dose of Mediterranean culture thrown in for good measure.

The Tel Aviv beachfront

The Dan Hotel's exterior is adorned with a hallmark multicolor design by artist Ya'akov Agam.

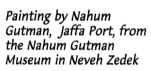

Painting by Nahum Gutman, Jaffa Port, from the Nahum Gutman Museum in Neveh Zedek

*Interior of the Tel
Aviv Opera House*

The Carmel Market

Dizengoff Center

Nahalat Benyamin pedestrian mall

Tiles by Tartakover in the Suzanna Dellal Center depicting the early history of Tel Aviv

*The Suzanne Dellal Center for Dance and Theater in Tel Aviv-Jaffa's
restored Neveh Zedek neighborhood*

Caesarea

When Herod the Great built the city of Caesarea in 20 BCE on the foundations of an ancient Phoenician town and named it in honor of his patron Caesar Augustus, he intended it to be his showcase to the world. In the best Roman tradition, aqueducts transported water to verdant courtyard gardens and fountains on elegant intersecting boulevards. Its population enjoyed performances at a 5000-seat theater, and cheered at the chariot races that took place in its gigantic stadium.

Caesarea's port was a technical marvel of its day. It was silt-free, despite the alluvial currents eddying northward from the River Nile, and a giant lighthouse probably illuminated the way to moorings located in two inner harbors behind artificial breakwaters. Here bustling offices and storehouses processed the valuable merchandise shipped in from across the sea, and exported the riches of Arabia westward.

Like other cities of the coastal plain, Jews, pagans and Samaritans, and eventually, Christians, lived side-by-side in Caesarea. But in this town that was eventually to become the Roman capital of Judea, life was not always peaceful. Josephus Flavius relates that a conflict between pagans and Jews in Caesarea was the spark that ignited the Great Revolt of 66 CE. Christianity made its first inroads here into the pagan world when Peter converted the gentile Cornelius the Centurion and his household here. Paul was a prisoner at Caesarea, having been arrested in Jerusalem and brought to appear before the Roman rulers in their headquarters here. He later set sail for Rome from the Caesarea port.

When Christianity took over the empire in the fourth century, Caesarea grew by leaps and bounds. Church scholar Eusebius was bishop of the town, and another outstanding Christian sage, Origen, taught here, attracting followers from far and wide.

Ancient fragments scattered on the sand west of the theater at Caesarea

The arches of Caesarea's ancient aqueduct span one of the country's most popular beaches.

In later years, the city's importance shrank considerably when overland routes took precedence over maritime trade. Caesarea made a brief comeback during the Crusader era when the Holy Grail was discovered here by the knights of Baldwin I. It was one of the last cities to fall into Muslim hands at the end of the era.

Fragments of monumental Roman statuary

The famous Pontius Pilate inscription unearthed in Caesarea's theater

A crusader tower is silhouetted against the backdrop of a Caesarea sunset

124

Artist's rendering of the inner port
of Herodian-era Caesarea

Excavations within the Crusader city

Herod's amphitheater

Caesarea National Park, looking north. At center is the theater built in Herod's day.

Mount Carmel

Statue of Elijah in the courtyard of the Mukhraka Monastery

Due to its altitude and proximity to the sea, Mount Carmel is one of the greenest spots in the Holy Land. The ancient inhabitants of the land attributed this bounty to blessings bestowed by the god of rain, Baal, and his consort, Ishtar. The Israelites, to the chagrin of biblical prophets, worshipped these deities. But Elijah was one prophet undeterred by the popularity of idol worship. On the contrary, he may have chosen Mount Carmel precisely because of its appeal to the Baal worshippers when he issued his challenge to the Baal's prophets to bring down fire from heaven.

In one of the Bible's most dramatic passages (1 Kings 18:19-39) God answers the prayer of Elijah with fire from heaven. The people abandon the Canaanite deities, and Elijah orders the priests of Baal slaughtered at the nearby brook of Kishon. Finally, a devastating drought ends with a thunderous downpour. The traditional site of the contest, now occupied by a Carmelite Monastery, bears the Arabic name "Mukhraka" which means the place of the burning.

View of Mount Carmel looking west towards the Mediterranean

The Carmel Caves National Park

The Mukhraka, traditional site of Elijah's contest with the prophets of Ba'al. At center, the Carmelite Monastery commemorating the event.

One of the newest Bahai buildings

Haifa

One of the few cities in Israel not mentioned in the Bible, Haifa owes its fame to the advent of the modern age. When the port at Acre became too small to support modern shipping, Haifa, a small Turkish town on the other side of the bay, and home since the seventeenth century to Carmelite monks, came into its own.

One of the first modern residential neighborhoods in the country was established here with the arrival in the late nineteenth century of the industrious German Christian sect known as the Templers.

The Bahai Shrine of the Bab and its magnificent terraces

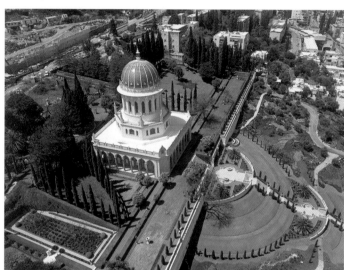

Haifa port by night

In 1909, Abdul Baha, son of the Baha'ullah, founder of the Bahai sect, (who had lived out his life under house arrest in Acre after being exiled from Persia by the Muslims) constructed a mausoleum on Mount Carmel sacred to the faith, in the new town of Haifa. Here, the remains of the Bab, who was the predecessor of the Baha'ullah and had been executed in 1850 Persia, were brought for reinternment.

With the arrival of the British, a modern port was constructed and Haifa became the economic hub it is today. Industries of all kinds set up shop in the bay area, as new residential neighborhoods climbed Mount Carmel. In 1925 Haifa entered the world of academe, with the establishment of the Technion, Israel's technical university.

Facade and interior of the Stella Maris Church

Monument over the tomb of Napoleon's soldiers who died in the 1799 siege of Acre

Shrine to Elijah in the Stella Maris Church

The Science Museum, housed in the first home of the Technion, Haifa's world-famous technical university, opened in 1924

Dagon, the Haifa Grain Silo

The Druse

The Druse faith grew out of Islam, originating in Egypt in the eleventh century. Like all faiths born after the advent of Muhammad, the Druse religion was not accepted by Islam, and to escape persecution, its adherents fled Egypt for other countries of the Middle East. Today, the majority of the adherents of this monotheistic religion live in Lebanon, Syria, and Israel.

The Druse faith is largely a mystic one, with many of its arcane aspects revealed only to the initiated, a status reached through moral excellence and selection by the community's elders. The Druse believe in reincarnation, giving rise to many fascinating stories told within the community of interconnected relationships spanning centuries and households.

The traditional dress of religious Druse men is distinctive by its pleated pantaloons and red tarboosh wrapped in white cloth. The older members of the community almost invariably sport a bushy handle-bar mustache as well. The women's traditional garb is a simple black dress with a white veil covering the hair.

One important tenet of the Druse culture is loyalty to the flag under which they live. Therefore Israel's Druse community are subject, at the request of the community's elders soon after the founding of the State, to compulsory draft into the armed forces. The Druse, numbering some 90,000, inhabit several towns on Mount Carmel and the Golan.

Restaurants and shops on the main street of the Druze town of Dalyat el-Carmel attract visitors from home and abroad.

Zichron Ya'akov

Founded in 1882, this farming community was taken under the wing of Baron Edmund de Rothschild, who named it in honor of his father James. The Carmel Wineries, founded here soon after, made the town famous.

Dozens of cannons once guarded Acre's ramparts

Acre

The unbeatable combination of battlements and a beautiful blue sea, make Acre one of the Holy Land's most charming locales. Mentioned in the ancient Egyptian El-Amarna letters, it was conquered in its day by Alexander the Great. It is a town well-known to Europeans, especially after Crusader Jerusalem's fall in 1187, when the city became the Crusader capital of the Holy Land.

First port of call for countless medieval pilgrims, the riches of Acre's markets and caravanserais were legendary; at the time of the 1191 Third Crusade, the economic output of Acre was greater than all of England!. Even after the 1291 fall of the Crusaders Europeans continued to frequent the Acre port, especially to export wheat from the Golan and the Galilee during the eighteenth-century rule of the region's enterprising Bedouin chieftain Daher el Omar.

In 1799, Napoleon besieged Acre in an attempt to further his conquests in the Middle East. He was roundly rebuffed at Acre by a carefully orchestrated Turkish-British alliance under command of wily octogenarian Ahmad Al-Jazzar ("The Butcher"). European interest in Acre persisted: In 1830, when Muhammad Ali of Egypt took control of Palestine, the British came to the aide of the Ottoman Turks to protect their strategic interests in the region, bombarding the city into submission.

Today's town is notable for its picturesque lanes and narrow back streets, some of them unchanged for 800 years. Its monuments and markets hum with visitors, reliving the rich history of Acre's days gone by.

The crowded houses and markets of Acre's old city follow a virtually untouched medieval street layout.

Interior of the Al-Jazzar Mosque

The Al-Jazzar Mosque by night

"St. John's Crypt" in Acre's Knights' Halls

The eighteenth century Khan el-Umdan, or "Inn of the Columns"

View of Acre from the east shows the attractions of Acre - ancient walls against the background of the sea.

Montfort

The ruins of Montfort Castle cling to a spur covered with the dense copses of scrub oak typical to the high mountains of Galilee. Overlooking the deep valley of Nahal Keziv, Montfort was the thirteenth-century home of the Teutonic order of St. Mary, who rebuilt the small fort that had previously occupied the site. A great deal of work was needed on the old fort, and the Master of the Teutonic order, Hermann von Salza, made a special appeal for funds to Pope Gregory IX.

Remains of the eighteenth century aqueduct that brought water to Acre from Galilee mountain springs

Achziv

This beautiful beach resort is one of Israel's most famous. Do these vacationers know they are relaxing in the shadow of one of the most ancient towns of the region, once a seacoast holding of the Tribe of Asher (Josh 19:29)?

Rosh HaNikra

The grottos of Rosh Hanikra were carved by wave action out of the bleached-white, flint-studded limestone ridge separating Israel from Lebanon known as "the Ladder of Tyre" (Macc 1:11;29). The caves, in and out of which the turquoise waters move incessantly, are accessible by cable-car and are connected to each other by artificial tunnels. A cryptic cement sign outside the grottos are all that is left to indicate that the British Army blasted out the adjacent railway tunnel for this section of the Haifa-Beirut railway in 1943. The tunnel was blown up by Palmach forces in March 1948, shortly before Israel's independence, to prevent the invasion of the Lebanese army via this strategic route.

Rosh HaNikra, whose caves are accessible by cable-car

The Jezreel Valley, Israel's breadbasket, is none other than the Book of Revelation's Valley of Armageddon, scene of the great battle of the End of Days.

Battles for the Jezreel began early in history as nations realized that domination of the valley was essential for control of the road traversing it that linked the two great kingdoms of antiquity, Egypt and Mesopotamia. The Bible relates that the Canaanites, thanks to their chariots, maneuvered successfully on the Jezreel's flat expanses, forcing the Israelites to take to the mountains. During the period of the Judges, the armies of Gideon and Deborah fought here, turning their command of the surrounding highlands against their better-equipped enemies.

Battles for the Jezreel continued right up until the modern age. Napoleon fought here in 1799 and Allenby in 1917. The border of the State of Israel in 1948 was drawn here at the point where Israelis successfully halted the Jordanian Legion's advance. From antiquity to the present, the strategic importance of the valley remained paramount.

Like much of the rest of the country, the Jezreel Valley suffered from neglect in the modern era; lying mostly uncultivated, its high water table turned it slowly to swamp. The Jezreel was one of the first areas of the country where land was purchased by Jewish pioneers, who transformed the swamp into the fertile farmland it is today.

The Jezreel Valley, with Mount Tabor

Mount Gilboa

Somewhere on this mountain range that separates the eastern reaches of the Jezreel Valley from the Jordan Valley, King Saul took his own life after his defeat at the hands of the Philistines, and the death of his three sons in battle. David laments the death of Saul and Jonathan with these immortal words: "Ye mountains of Gilboa, let there be no dew, neither let there be rain upon you, nor fields of offerings. For there the shield of the mighty is vilely cast away...How are the mighty fallen in battle! O Jonathan, thou wast slain in thine high places" (2 Samuel 1:21-25).

*Celebrating a holiday
kibbutz-style*

The Kibbutz

The Kibbutz way of life—the word means collective—began with the founding of the first such community, Kinneret, some ninety years ago on the shores of the Sea of Galilee. Young Jewish pioneers, mainly hailing from pre-revolutionary Russia, sought to combine the ideals of social justice and equality then coming to the fore with a return to their ancestral homeland in the Land of Israel to work the land and create a new society.

Over the years, the kibbutz has become uniquely identified with Israel. But though it is arguably one of the most significant social movements of the twentieth century, its adherents number only about 124,000—about 2.2 per cent of Israel's population—living in some 270 communities averaging a few hundred families each.

But the kibbutz has contributed far more than its share to the shaping of Israeli society, and to its very existence. Some 33 per cent of Israel's agricultural products are of kibbutz origin, as well as about 8% of the country's industry. In the early years of the kibbutz movement, the willingness of its members to inhabit hostile locations aided in the defense of the country. As well, the centralized

A Jordan Valley kibbutz

community life and strong ideological commitment of kibbutz members made it natural to call upon them as a group to aid in the absorption of countless newcomers after the establishment of the State.

As modern life brings about the need for economic and social reforms throughout society, many of the hallmarks of kibbutz life, the sleep-away childrens' houses, the dining room, and the traditional community meeting for example, are now being transformed to suit the new generation. Even the very basis of kibbutz society, that no member should receive a salary beyond that of another, have undergone reevaluation. It remains to be seen what this most Israeli of Israeli institutions will be in the new millennium.

Kibbutz children hard at work in the classroom

Lion seal discovered at Megiddo, bearing the name of Jeroboam King of Israel

Megiddo

From earliest times, an incessant stream of warriors and traders passed beneath the walls of Megiddo, the town that straddles the most important junction of the road through the Jezreel Valley.

Megiddo is the site of history's first recorded battle: in 1468 CE Pharaoh Thutmose III came to return control of the region to the Egyptians, fighting a coalition of Canaanite insurgents. He took the enemy by surprise by following an unexpected route from the sea coast to the Jezreel Valley. However, because his men turned to sacking the rich villages of the valley, it took him a further seven months to subdue the town!.

Excavations at Megiddo have revealed not only the very gates that barred entrance to Thutmose's army, but also the extensive building activities of King Solomon in the town, including the palace from which his son-in-law, Ba'anah, ruled the district. Megiddo's water tunnel, built during the days of Ahab, brought spring water into a well in the midst of the town in an attempt to create a siege-proof city. Eventually, the city succumbed to the Assyrians during their 721 BCE incursion.

Twenty-five layers of civilization make Megiddo one of the most significant historical and archaeological sites in Israel. Moreover, its strategic location and the numerous battles fought within sight of it, inspired the writer of the Book of Revelations to lend its name, in Greek form, to the surrounding valley as the site of the greatest battle of all, the apocalyptic Armageddon.

The round Canaanite altar where animal sacrifices were performed

Steps descending to a water system beneath the town's solomonic gateway

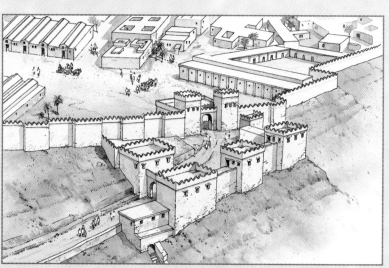

Artist's rendering of the city gate and environs during King Solomon's time

This menorah decorated the interior of one of Beit Shearim's rock-cut tombs

Megiddo's eighth century BCE central grain silo

Beit Shearim

Beit Shearim became a focal point of Jewish life in the second century CE, after the failed Bar-Kokhba Revolt (132-135) forced the move of Jews from Judea northward to the Galilee. The town was the seat of the Sanhedrin, Judaism's highest judicial-religious authority of the time.

At the head of the Sanhedrin stood Rabbi Judah the Prince, compiler of the Mishna (the commentary on the Bible and the earliest part of the Talmud). When illness necessitated his move to the more salubrious Sepporis to the north, the Sanhedrin moved too. But upon his death in 220, the famed luminary's remains were interred at Beit Shearim. From then on, Jews the world over requested burial at Beit Shearim to be near Rabbi Judah. The town flourished until its destruction by the Romans in 352 after revolt broke out against Gallus Caesar.

A synagogue and more than thirty burial caverns have been discovered at the site, now a national park. Within the caverns are numerous intricately carved and inscribed sarcophagi (stone coffins), providing a wealth of information about burial customs during this pivotal period of Jewish history.

Present-day exit from the tunnel dug in the days of Ahab

Entrance courtyard of a Beit Shearim tomb complex

The Galilee

Mount Tabor

Mount Tabor's curvaceous symmetry and oak-blanketed slopes make it the most outstanding geographical feature of the Jezreel Valley. The 588 meter-high mountain figured centrally in the story of Deborah, who instructed her general, Barak, to lead his troops to the mountain. When the over-confident Canaanite general Sisera and his nine hundred chariots reached the vicinity, Barak and his army swept down from Mount Tabor to attack and defeat them (Judges 4:14-15).

As the lyric "Song of Deborah" (Judges 5) records: "And the princes of Issachar were with Deborah; even Issachar and also Barak: he was sent on foot into the valley...The kings came and fought, then fought the kings of Canaan in Ta'anach by the waters of Megiddo; they took no gain of money. They fought from heaven; the stars in their courses fought against Sisera. "

Aerial view of the church and monastery on Mount Tabor

Later, fourth century pilgrim Egeria became the first to identify Tabor as the "high mountain" of the Transfiguration of Jesus (Matt.17:2-3). Since the Byzantine period, a church has marked the spot of the Transfiguration. The present church, refurbished at the beginning of the twentieth century, is graced with impressive stonework and magnificent mosaics depicting the Transfiguration and its symbolism.

The Greek Orthodox Church

Detail from the Church of the Transfiguration

Nain

"...he went to a town called Nain, accompanied by his disciples and a great number of people. When he was near the gate of the town, it happened that a dead man was being carried out for burial, the only sone of his mother, and she was a widow...Then [Jesus] went up and put his hand on the bier...and he said, "Young man, I tell you, get up. And the dead man sat up and began to talk, and Jesus gave him to his mother (Luke 7:11-15).

Interior of the present-day Church of the Transfiguration

Facade of the Church of the Transfiguration

Church of the Annunciation

Nazareth

Christianity has much love for this city where Mary received the news that she would give birth to Jesus and where Jesus spent his formative years. Interestingly, the New Testament has few references to the life Jesus led here, and scholars commonly refer to this time as "the silent years".

Over the centuries, pilgrims have associated numerous sites around the city with the life of Jesus and with Mary. Fourth-century pilgrim Egeria writes in her diary that she saw the grotto where the Annunciation to Mary was made by the angel Gabriel. This is likely the same grotto pilgrims view today within the Roman Catholic Basilica of the Annunciation.

The apocryphal gospel of James adds a descriptive detail to the story of the Annunciation: He reports that the angel appeared to Mary as she drew water from the well, a task she no doubt performed daily together with the other young women of the village. In the Crusader era, a church was built over the site closest to the point of emanation of the spring of Nazareth. That church, the Church of Saint Gabriel, is the center of the town's

Grotto of the Annunciation

The city of Nazareth, with the conical-domed Basilica of the Annunciation at center

vibrant Greek Orthodox community and a revered focus of pilgrimage.

Perhaps the most dramatic event recorded in the gospels pertaining to Jesus in Nazareth is recorded by Luke. During Jesus' sermon in the Nazareth synagogue, the people of the city became incensed against him, chasing him out of town. Just as they were about to push him off a cliff, he, "passing through the midst of them, went on his way" (Luke 4:30).

That cliff, called the Mount of Precipitation, is also known as the Mount of Trembling, because legend has it that Mary stood nearby trembling at what she presumed would be the fate of her son.

Christians of nearly all persuasions reside in Nazareth; clergy hailing from around the world serve in the city's monasteries and convents devoting their lives to teaching, healing, and contemplation.

The Annunciation

Crusader capital and statue fragment unearthed in excavations on the site of the present-day Basilica of the Annunciation

Caves were used for storage in the Nazareth of Jesus' day

Detail of the Zodiac

144

Courtyard of the Greek Orthodox Church of St. Gabriel

Newly refurbished Nazareth market street

Mary's Well by David Roberts, 1839

Mary's Well in the Church of St. Gabriel

St. Joseph's Church

Interior of Nazareth's Synagogue Church,
on the site where Jesus preached

The Holy Family,
statue outside St.
Joseph's Church

View of the Jezreel Valley from the Mount of Precipitation east of Nazareth

Cana

Cana is the site of the first miracle of Jesus, as recorded by John's gospel. "...there was a marriage in Cana of in Galilee; and the mother of Jesus was there: And both Jesus was called, and his disciples to the marriage. And when they wanted wine, the mother of Jesus said to him 'they have no more wine'...And there were set there six stone water pots, after the manner of the purifying of the Jews containing two or three firkins apiece. Jesus saith unto them fill the water pots with water. And they filled them up to the brim. And he saith unto them, draw out and bear unto the governor of the feast. And they bare it. When the ruler of the feast had tasted the water that was made wine and knew not whence it was." (John 2:1-9).

A Roman Catholic church in Cana stands over the site where a mosaic reveals that a synagogue stood during Roman times. In those days, the synagogue was a likely place for a wedding banquet to be held. Among Cana's other churches is one dedicated to Nathaniel, the disciple of Jesus who was a native of this town.

Mosaic dedication inscription in the Wedding Church, dating from the fifth century synagogue that once stood here.

Cana's churches. At left, the red domes of the Wedding Church. At right, a chapel dedicated to Philip.

Life in the
Times of Jesus

Sepphoris

Jesus could have walked in an hour from Nazareth to Sepphoris and many scholars have come to believe he probably did. Josephus records that Herod the Great, during his campaign to take control of the country, captured Sepphoris in a snowstorm. Herod's son Antipas built Sepphoris to serve as the capital of the region after his father's death. Josephus called this city "the greatest city in all Galilee".

Later, Sepphoris gained prominence as seat of the Sanhedrin, the Jewish Council, during the time of the compilation of the Mishnah by Rabbi Judah the Prince. The city achieved fame in Christian lore as the birthplace of Mary.

Joseph and Jesus, carpenters by trade—some scholars believe the original Greek word denotes work in the building trades in general—may well have plied their trade in this city so close to their own village. Archaeologists have found a 4000-seat theater here, numerous streets laid out in grid formation, and an impressive rock-hewn water system. The number of magnificent mosaics that continues to be unearthed here is unparalleled anywhere in Israel. Scholars utilize these discoveries to take a new look at the cultural context of Jesus' teachings. They note that in addition to the well-known "rustic" parables, Jesus set many of his homilies in an urban background and wonder if Sepphoris might have been the "big city" that Jesus drew upon for his illustrations.

Monastery of St. Anne, mother of Mary, on the traditional remains of her house

View of the excavations of Sepphoris. On the left, a Crusader-era watch- tower. Right, restored house containing the famous "Mona Lisa of the Galilee" mosaic

Aramaic mosaic inscription which reads: "Honored be the memory of Rabbi Yudan son of Butah, who made the mosaic, may it be for him a blessing." The inscription, possibly from a third century CE synagogue, was unearthed in the nineteenth century.

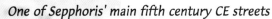

One of Sepphoris' main fifth century CE streets

A portion of the tunnel that channeled spring water from the hills of Nazareth to Sepphoris

The "Mona Lisa of the Galilee"; detail of a mosaic that decorated a floor in a third-century CE Sepphoris home.

The Sea of Galilee

The Sea of Galilee is the catchment basin for the Jordan River, whose origins are the melting snows of Mount Hermon to the north. Numerous other seasonal streams flow down from the surrounding mountains to this low-lying, fresh-water lake, 206 meters below sea level.

The Lake is 25 kilometers long and 14 kilometers wide, 50 meters deep, with a surface area of 165 square kilometers. But the Sea of Galilee is so much more than the sum of its vital statistics! In a land so barren, this fresh-water lake provides much needed greenery, respite for the eyes and the soul and, through the intense cultivation possible here, nourishment for the body. "One may call this place the ambition of nature", wrote Josephus, "where it forces those plants that are naturally enemies to one another to agree together".

The ancients waxed poetic when they named the lake. They called it Kinneret

The Sea of Galilee, looking west

which means "lyre", because its shape reminded them of that musical instrument played by King David and by the Levites in the Temple. The lake lies deep in a crevice created by earthquakes. Those same earth movements resulted in the appearance of hot sulfur springs around the shore, to which for centuries the ill have flocked to be cured of their maladies.

Jesus spent most of his three-year public ministry in towns and villages around the Sea of Galilee. Some scholars, taking note of the large number of sick people that came to Jesus to be healed, believe that they may have initially come to the region to take advantage of the hot springs.

Artist's rendering of the Ancient Galilee Boat

The Ancient Galilee Boat

The discovery in 1986 of this ancient vessel, mired in the mud near Magdala on the northwest shore of the Sea of Galilee, caused a stir throughout the world, especially after it was conclusively dated to the fateful first century CE, the time both of Jesus and the Great Revolt of the Jews against the Romans. The boat, made primarily of cedar and oak, is now on exhibit at Kibbutz Ginnosar. It is 9 meters long, 2.5 meters wide, and 1.25 meters high. It may have functioned as a ferry boat, but its measurements also suit use by ancient fishermen employing a seine, or dragnet, "cast into the sea" as described in Matt 13:47-48.

Tiberias

Tiberias, capital of the lake region today, was founded by Herod Antipas in about 22 CE and named for the Emperor Tiberius. The city is mentioned in the New Testament only as a name of the lake. Was this splendid city, with its healing hot springs, ever visited by Jesus?

Herod Antipas had desired to build a new Roman-style city in this subtropical location. But in chosing a location occupied by a Jewish cemetery, he antagonized many potential residents who viewed the city's cemetery-location as a desecration of the dead and a violation of Jewish law. It is possible that Jesus was among the many who would not set foot in the city.

In later years, the city shook off its inferior reputation. People flocked to the hot springs, prompting a talmudic discussion as to the propriety of bathing in them on the Sabbath day (permissible, it was decided, for medicinal but not recreational purposes). The Sanhedrin, the Jewish council, was quartered here for a time, and the Gemara, the second book of the Talmud, was compiled here. The city eventually became a magnet for Jewish pilgrims, many of whom came to pay homage to the memory of the great Spanish twelfth century sage Maimonides, interred here.

Christians, too, lived in the city. After the Persian and Muslim conquests when many of their churches were destroyed, they continued to pray in a magnificent church high above the city at the site now known as Mount Bereniki. During the Crusader and the Middle Ages the ancient walls of Tiberias were restored, and their remains can still be seen today.

The ancient Tiberias hot springs

Remains of the Arbel synagogue

Arbel

The Arbel cliff towers above the main road linking the region of central Galilee to the Sea of Galilee, and points north. When, as Matthew writes, Jesus left Nazareth and "came and dwelt in Capernaum which is upon the sea coast..."(Matt 4:13), this is the road that he would have traveled.

Some three decades before the birth of Jesus, a terrible scene played itself out here. Josephus provides the horrific details: Jewish opponents to the rule of Herod the Great took to the caves that riddle the rocks here. The threat to this important main artery posed by the insurgents proved too much for the new sovereign. Unable to reach them by any other means, Herod ordered his soldiers to arm themselves with huge hooks, and lower themselves inside of great cages from the edge of the cliff above the rebels' hideouts. When they reached the cave openings, they pulled out the rebels with the hooks and flung them into the gorge beneath. Josephus describes how some of the trapped Jews preferred to throw themselves or their families into the gorge rather than meet their death at the hands of the enemy.

Magdala

Home town of Mary Magdalene, Magdala was one of many Jewish fishing villages along the Sea of Galilee shores. Its name means "tower", probably referring to a light-house which guided ancient fishermen home.

The Arbel Cliff

Tabgha

Early Christians named the traditional site of the first multiplication of loaves and fishes (Matt. 14:13-21) "Heptapegon", which means seven springs, after seven water sources that flow into the Sea of Galilee here. Today, the name has been shortened in the Arabic pronunciation to "Tabgha".

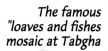

Near the altar of the present-day church is a mosaic panel dating back some 1500 years, depicting the basket of loaves and two fishes with which Jesus fed the multitudes who had come to hear him preach. Beneath the altar, a piece of bedrock protrudes: tradition deems it here that Jesus "...looking up to heaven...blessed, and baoke, and gave the loaves to his disciples, and the disciples to the multitude." (Matt. 14:19)

A later church built here under the direction of Matyrius, a bishop from Egypt, continued the mosaic tradition. His legacy: the exquisite array of Nile-region flora and fauna that still graces the floor. A community of Benedictine Monks now maintains the site and runs a camp for handicapped children on the nearby lake shore.

Meditation spot at Dalmanutha (Mark 8:10) near Tabgha

Courtyard of the Church of the Multiplication

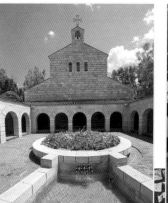

The famous "loaves and fishes mosaic at Tabgha

The Church of Peter's Primacy

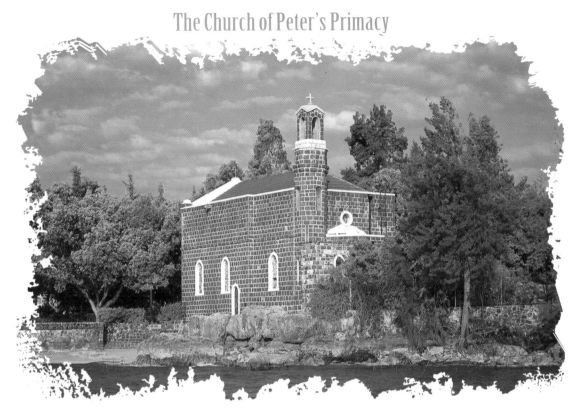

The Church of Peter's Primacy is named for the events of John 21. Here Jesus charges Peter with the care of the Church, with the famous words "feed my lambs...feed my sheep" (John 21:15-17).

Another name for this Franciscan holy place is "Mensa Christi" which means "Table of Christ". Its name refers to the preparation by Jesus of a meal of bread and fish for the disciples when he appeared to them after the resurrection. Peter and some of the disciples had been fishing, unsuccessfully, all that night. When they were about to come ashore, Jesus, whom at first they did not recognize ordered them to cast their net on the other side of the boat, where they caught so many fish that the net could not be lifted up (John 21:1-14).

Statue of Peter kneeling before Jesus at the Church of Peter's Primacy

Capernaum

Capernaum was the center of Jesus' Galilee ministry. He taught in its synagogue and cast out the demons plaguing a man of the town (Mark 1:21-28). In connection with the synagogue we also meet a Roman officer who resided in the town. It is not surprising to find Roman soldiers garrisoned in the city: Capernaum was on the border between the two administrative regions of Galilee and Golan, and taxes were collected here that would have needed imperial guards.(Matthew, known as Levi, was a tax collector in Capernaum.) The nameless Roman officer, like Cornelius of Caesarea, was a righteous gentile; in Luke 7:5, Jesus' disciples note the centurion "loveth our nation and hath built us a synagogue", and Jesus was persuaded to heal his servant.

It was also in Capernaum that Jesus healed Peter's mother-in-law of a fever (Mark 1:21).

Once, when Jesus was preaching in one of the homes of the town, such a crowd gathered that not one more person could crowd into the house. But Capernaum's citizens would not give up: in order to allow a paralytic to enter, they must have had to cut a hole in the roof (probably made of mud and straw) above Jesus in order to lower the man through

The fifth-century synagogue of Capernaum

Olive oil press discovered in ancient Capernaum

Capernaum dwellings from Jesus' day, with the St. Peter Memorial in the background

the opening! (Mark 2:1-4).

Extensive excavations have been carried out in Capernaum under the auspices of the Franciscans, owners of the property since the late nineteenth century. They have discovered remains of a fifth century synagogue, the earlier synagogue from Jesus' day that lies beneath it, as well as the ruins of a Byzantine Church built around what is believed to have been the house of Peter. Homes and courtyards from the time of Jesus have also been found. All of these discoveries bring alive numerous New Testament stories and make Capernaum an essential part of pilgrims' itineraries.

The Greek Orthodox Church of Capernaum

Aerial view of Capernaum

The Mount of Beatitudes

The most important collection of Jesus' Galilee teachings are known as the Sermon on the Mount. The sermon is believed to have been delivered on the Mount of Beatitudes, named for the nine times (in the account of Matthew) Jesus begins a sentence with the words "blessed" (in Latin, beati).

Although the most oft-quoted version of the Sermon on the Mount comes from Matthew 5, it is in the Gospel of Luke that we find a geographical description that fits this traditional site of the Mount of Beatitudes: "...Jesus went out into a mountain to pray, and continued all night in prayer to God. And when it was day, he called unto him his disciples: and of them he chose twelve...and he came down with them, and stood in the plain..." (Luke 6:12-17).

Standing on the top of the Mount of Beatitudes, with a plateau stretching out below just as described in Luke, it is easy to imagine this as the place where Jesus prayed and chose the Twelve before descending to the "plain" to preach to the

The Church of the Beatitudes

multitudes. The present church, built by the Italians, dates from the twentieth century. It stands upon remains of churches from earlier periods, a sign that homage has been paid to this spot for centuries.

The Beatitudes

Blessed are the poor in spirit, for theirs is the kingdom of Heaven.

Blessed are they that mourn, for they shall be comforted.

Blessed are the meek: for they shall inherit the earth.

Blessed are they which do hunger and thirst after righteousness: for they shall be filled.

Blessed are the merciful: for they shall obtain mercy.

Blessed are the pure in heart: for they shall see God.

Blessed are the peacemakers: for they shall be called the children of God.

Blessed are they which are persecuted for righteousness' sake: for theirs is the kingdom of heaven. (Matthew 5:3-10)

Portico of the Church of the Beatitudes, looking west

Interior of the Church of the Beatitudes

Korazin

The distinctive black basalt carvings at Korazin's synagogue shed light on both the artistic preferences and the financial means of the fourth century Jewish community that commissioned them. Among the finds in archaeological excavations here: a stone-carved "seat of Moses" - the preacher's chair. In this chair would sit the person upon whom the honor of reading and expounding on the law had been conferred. Jesus would have sat in a chair like this when he preached in the synagogue of Nazareth and Capernaum. Jesus mentions a seat of Moses in Matthew 23:2.

Bethsaida

The hometown of both Peter and Philip, Bethsaida, is located near the north shore of the Sea of Galilee. Here Jesus healed a blind man (Mark 8:22). Of the town Jesus said, "Woe unto thee, Bethsaida! For if the mighty works which were done in you had been done in Tyre and Sidon, they would have repented long ago in sackcloth and ashes." (Matthew 11:21)

Tel Bethsaida in the Jordan River delta

The partially restored Korazim synagogue

Kursi

"And they came over unto the other side of the sea, into the country of the Gadarenes. And when he was come out of the ship, immediately there met him out of the tombs a man with an unclean spirit. ...Now there was therer nigh unto the mountains a great herd of swine feeding. And all the devils besought him, saying send us into the swine that we may enter into them. And forthwith Jesus gave them leave. And the unclean spirits went out, and entered into the swine: and the herd ran violently down a steep place into the sea."(Mark 5:1-13)

Each of the synoptic gospels reports these events, known as the "miracle of the swine", in a slightly different version. Even the name of the place is different in each of the three accounts: in one place the land of the Gerasenes, and in another, the land of the Gadarenes. In the course of history, therefore, sites as far afield as Jerash and Gadara in Jordan were seen as the locale of the miracle. Gergesa, a town probably on the same location as the site known as Kursi today, but later abandoned, is named as the place of the miracle in some versions of Luke. Kursi is close enough to the lake

to fit the dramatic description of the rush of the herd of swine "down a steep place into the sea..."(Mark 5:13).

Not long ago, while road works were in progress on the east side of the lake, a heretofore unknown Byzantine church and monastery were discovered at Kursi demonstrating an early Christian affinity to the site which many believe to be the long-lost Gergesa.

The restored Byzantine church at Kursi

The Jordan River Park

The Jordan River flows into the Sea of Galilee from its northern shore, creating a lush delta which is home to hundreds of species of birds and a favorite stop for bird-watchers from around the world.

Ein Gev

Kibbutz Ein Gev, founded on the eastern shore of the Sea of Galilee in 1937, is well-known for its guest house and fish restaurant which specializes in the lake's famed St. Peter's fish (*tilapia*), as well as for its bananas and dates. The Kibbutz Ein Gev concert hall hosts dozens of cultural events each year. Its small museum, "The Anchor House", founded by kibbutz member Mendel Nun, an expert in local lore, specializes in fishing techniques as they are reflected in the New Testament stories and parables. Over the years, Ein Gev's fleet of boats has ferried countless pilgrims across the lake.

Hamat Gader

On the banks of the Yarmuk River close to the Israel-Jordan b Border, the sulphur springs of Hamat Gader have long been famous for their curative powers. Legend has it that Paul the Apostle himself bathed in these waters. Todays visitors seek out Hamat Gader to luxuriate in its warm waters, explore the ruins, and enjoy a visit to its alligator farm and small zoo.

Ruins of Susita

Susita

Some scholars believe that Susita, on a rocky outcropping towering above its surroundings, was the city meant by Jesus when he said "A city on a hill cannot be hidden. "(Matthew 5:14)

Kibbutz Ein Gev, with the hill of Susita in the background

Yardenit

The Jordan River is the most important body of water in Judaeo-Christian tradition. This is the river that Joshua and the Children of Israel crossed, its waters miraculously "piling up" so they could traverse on dry land. Later, Elijah and Elisha also caused the waters to stop flowing (2 Kings 2:8). In these waters Na'aman the Syrian was healed of his leprosy (2 Kings 5:14). And, of course, this was the river in which Jesus was baptized by John (Matthew 3:13-17).

Scriptural evidence points to the place of the Baptism of Jesus in the Jordan near the wilderness of Judea in the south. But the Jordan River is the line of demarcation between Israel and Jordan, and until recently border tensions made visits to the ancient church on that site nearly impossible.

During those years it became the custom of pilgrims to visit the Jordan at this northern locale, near the point where it exits the Sea of Galilee. Here, comfortable facilities are now maintained for pilgrims who wish to be baptized or renew baptismal vows.

View of Safed, with Mount Meron in the background

Safed

High in the Galilee mountains, Safed is home to Kabbalah, Jewish mysticism. Priestly families who escaped Jerusalem's destruction with the fall of the Second Temple once lived here, and the town maintained its Jewish community through centuries when it was no more than a sleepy mountain hamlet diffidently ruled by Byzantines, Fatimid Caliphs, Crusaders and Mameluke Turks.

With the rise of the Ottoman Turks, the city awakened. Weaving and printing industries moved to the town. Its population increased as refugee sages and scholars flocked here from Spain and Portugal after the 1492 Inquisition, seeking to be close to the grave of Second Temple-era sage Rabbi Shimon Bar Yohai, author of the famed mystic work, the Zohar— "The Splendor".

Jewish mysticism seeks the answers to the eternal questions posed by people of faith. In their search, kabbalists look deeply into what they call the "secret wisdom" of the Bible which resides, they believe, beyond the literal meaning of the words. To reach this secret wisdom, the mystics' prayer becomes meditation, their study sessions a delving into esoteric realms such as the numerical value of the Hebrew words and even the very shape of the letters. By such methods the Jewish mystic furthers the sacred goal of comprehending the will of God.

Safed street scene

Remains of the ancient Meron synagogue

Meron

On the slope of one of Israel's highest mountains (1208 meters above sea level) is the grave of Rabbi Simeon Bar Yohai. Student of the famed Rabbi Akiva, Bar Yohai survived the Bar Kokhba revolt by hiding, according to talmudic legend, with his son, in a cave. On Lag Ba'omer, the traditional death date of Simeon Bar Yohai, thousands of Jews make a colorful pilgrimage to his tomb, where it is customary among certain communities to celebrate the first haircut of three year-old boys.

Bar'am

Facade of the Bar'am synagogue

Two synagogues graced this Galilee hilltop town in the third century CE. The better preserved of the two, pictured above, is now a national park, and was first described by a Jewish pilgrim in 1211. The third through the seventh centuries was a period of Jewish renaissance in the Galilee, and many synagogues were established. While the interior of the Bar'am synagogue is similar to others in the region, its elaborate facade was fronted by a colonnaded portico, the only Galilee synagogue so adorned.

The tomb of Rabbi Jonathan the Shoemaker at Meron. In the background is the famed tomb of Rabbi Simeon Bar Yohai

Tel Hazor

Hazor

At 200 acres, Tell Hazor is the largest tell in Israel. Its huge size hints at its importance; the town's influence in Bible days merited a particularly bitter fate during Joshua's conquest. The Book of Joshua relates:" And Joshua at that time turned back, and took Hazor, and smote the king thereof with the sword: for Hazor beforetime was the head of all those kingdoms. And they smote all the souls that were therein with the edge of the sword, utterly destroying them: there was not any left to breathe: and he burnt Hazor with fire"(Joshua 11:10-11). In the generations that followed, the city continued to be central to the rulers of the land, with King Solomon rebuilding it as a key to control of his northern domains.

Lion orthostat from Hazor, 14th-13th century BCE. Israel Museum

Hazor is mentioned numerous times in the great archives of the ancient Near East, the Egyptian Al-Amarna letters and the Assyrian Mari documents. Clearly, the town was a major player in the economic and political life of the Fertile Crescent. Generations of archaeologists have plumbed the depths of Hazor. Although they have unearthed remains of the Canaanites, Solomon's era, the period of the Israelite Kings, and the Assyrian destruction, it is believed that many of Hazor's secrets are still to be revealed.

The Hula Valley

The Hula Nature Reserve

"Yea, the stork in the heaven knoweth her appointed times, and the turtle and the crane and the swallow observe the time of their coming" (Jeremiah 8:7) said Jeremiah. In Jeremiah's day, as in our own, bird migration in the Holy Land skies is a thrilling seasonal spectacle. Israel is a bird-watcher's paradise, and the Hula Valley's 250-acre lake in the Hula Nature Reserve—a remnant of the much larger wetlands that existed here in the past until drained to permit cultivation—is center stage. Some 170 species of birds frequent the Hula in their bi-annual journey between Africa and Europe. (All told, some 400 species pass through Israel, with an incredible total of 500 million birds per year!) Cranes, storks, pelicans, spotted eagles, imperial eagles, pallid harriers and pygmy cormorants are among the feathered visitors taking advantage of the perfect conditions offered in the Hula Reserve to rest on their long journey between continents.

Vews of the Hula Reserve

Manara Cliff cablecar, looking towards Kiryat Shemonah

The Hula Valley

In the late nineteenth century, Jewish pioneers first came to settle the Hula Valley on land purchased at first by the well-known philanthropist Baron Edmund de Rothschild, and later on land acquired by the Jewish National Fund. These settlement ventures succeeded against all odds, as the land was inundated by swamps which were plagued with malarial mosquitoes that claimed many lives in the early years. As well, the small number of local people who inhabited the region viewed the newcomers with suspicion, especially after the advent of the great powers following World War One, and were often hostile.

The draining of the Hula Swamp in the 1950's produced sought-after fertile farmland, but resulted in various unexpected ecological repercussions including the loss of some wildlife habitat. Recently, an area adjacent to the Hula Nature Reserve has been reflooded in an attempt to restore nature's balance. In other areas, cotton, sunflowers, peanuts, chickpeas, plums and other crops blanket the valley, while the region's major towns, Kiryat Shemona and Metulla, continue to expand.

The Roaring Lion

This monument was erected over the grave of Joseph Trumpeldor, who died, together with seven other farmer-defenders of nearby Tel Hai, in 1920. Neighboring Kiryat Shemonah, "town of the eight", was named for them.

Metulla, with Mount Hermon in the background

2

170

Tel Dan

Dotted with gnarled old oak trees, Tel Dan sits in the midst of a nature reserve through which a sparkling river flows, one of the sources of the Jordan.

A haven of natural beauty, it is a paradise for Bible lovers, too. At the now-restored Israelite city gate, kings and

counselors of long-ago Dan would have pronounced their judgments. Israelite priests officiated for some 250 years at Dan's High Place beginning from the day King Jeroboam set up a golden calf there and made Dan

Tel Dan's Israelite city wall

the capital of the northern kingdom. A huge mud-brick gateway containing the world's oldest arch has been dated to the eighteenth century BCE, the patriarchal period. Abraham himself may have stood here: "And when Abram heard that his brother had been taken captive, he armed his trained servants born in his household, three hundred and eighteen, and pursued them unto Dan." (Gen 14:14).

The Dan River

"Abraham's Gate" at Dan, an eighteenth century BCE city gate

View of Dan's High Place

Caesarea Philipi - Banias

When Jesus and the disciples "came into the region of Caesarea Philipi" (Matt. 16:13), what did they see? A fruitful glen, through which a rushing river flowed, with the opulent residences, colonnaded streets and gigantic temples of a Roman city gleaming from its slopes.

The town was founded in the days of the Greeks and dedicated to the nature deity Pan and known as Panias. It was renamed in the Roman era by Herod Philip, son of Herod the Great, for himself and for Augustus Caesar, his family's patron. Here, surrounded by the excesses of pagan culture, Jesus asked his disciples the fateful question "whom do men say that I the Son of Man is?" (Matt 16:13), and renamed Simon as Peter, "the rock" on which the Church would be built. Recent excavations suggest that Caesarea Philipi was expanded on an even grander scale by King Agrippa II (the same monarch before whom Paul appeared in Acts 25).

The present name dates from the seventh-century Arab conquest and back to the ancient Greek name Panias. Lacking the letter P in their alphabet, Arab pronunciation became "Banias".

Remains of the Shrine of Pan at Banias

The Golan Heights

Mount Hermon

"Mount Hermon is the father of all the water"; so it was said in the early days of this century. This huge massif that lies partly in Israel, and partly in Lebanon and Syria, towers above the Golan Heights to its southeast and the Upper Galilee mountains on the west. At an altitude of 2814 meters, the rain and snow it receives are the single most important factor influencing the water system of the region.

The bounty of nature inherent in such abundant water was elevated to lyrical heights in Psalm 88 which says "Tabor and Hermon sing your praises". And the preciousness of brotherhood is considered as important as the precipitation from these snowy heights which Psalm 133 calls, "the dew of Hermon."

Skiing on Mount Hermon

View of the Nimrod Fortress with Mount Hermon in the background

The Sa'ar Waterfall

The Sa'ar Waterfall cascades from on high in the northern Golan Heights, where erosion-resistant basalt and frequent winter rain and snowfalls create a unique natural environment.

The Nimrod Fortress

The Nimrod Fortress is perched on a spur in the foothills of Mount Hermon, high above the all-important artery connecting the Land of Israel with Damascus. First built by the Crusaders in 1129, the fortress was handed over to the Muslims fifty years later. After one more try to restore Crusader control to the fortress in 1173, it was left to the Muslims. The curious name of the fortress derives from the Arabic legend that its first builder was Nimrod, the "mighty hunter" of Genesis 10:9.

174

The Golan Heights

Golan in the Bible appears as the name of one of the "cities of refuge" that fell within the tribal allotment of Manasseh in the area that the Bible calls Bashan. The most salient feature of its landscape is a series of volcanic craters in its northern sector. Lava flows from these volcanoes, long extinct, produced the basalt plateau now known as the Golan, a wedge-shaped territory some seventy kilometers long and twenty-five kilometers across, towering some 800 meters above the Sea of Galilee.

A shrine marks the traditional site of Abraham's vision of a smoking torch and a blazing firepot that "passed between the pieces" (Gen. 15:17).

Until 1967, the Syrian Army maintained well-defended gun emplacements on the Golan Heights, which were finally conquered by Israel in the Six-Day War in 1967. Soon afterwards, surveys by archaeologists, botanists, and zoologists revealed a region rich in both natural beauty and history. Clear waterfalls plunge dozens of meters from the hard basalt rock, home to coneys, gazelles and vultures, as well as wolves, foxes and other wildlife. Numerous ancient sites have been unearthed in the area, including synagogues and other remains left by the Jewish community that flourished in the area from the second to the seventh centuries. Todays population in the Golan numbers some twenty thousand, among them some seven thousand in the town of Katzrin, and the rest in kibbutzim, moshavim and Druse towns.

View of Susita and the Sea of Galilee from the western edge of the Golan Heights

Gamla

Gamla was a thriving town in an unusual location—on a seemingly inaccessible ridge shaped like a camel's back (Gamla means camel in Aramaic). At the beginning of the Great Revolt of the Jews against the Romans, Agrippa II, great-grandson of Herod the Great and ruler of the region, sided with the Romans against the rebels and attempted to subdue the town. But it was Roman General—later

The remains of the first century CE Gamla synagogue

Emperor—Vespasian at the head of three legions who finally vanquished the town after a constructing seven-month siege. The seige ended in bloody hand-to-handcombat between the town's residents and the Roman soldiers. After penetrating the town walls, the Romans forced them to flee to the top of the town which it overlooked an abyss. Rather than die an ignominious death at the hands of the conqueror, many residents of the town preferred to leap to their deaths. For this reason, Gamla is sometimes known as "the Massada of the North". Many elements of the siege have come to light in excavations, as well as as the town's synagogue.

Katzrin

The mishnaic era (second century CE) village of Katzrin has been partially restored, including the community's synagogue, pictured below.

The Meshushim Pool

The hard volcanic rock of the Golan Heights cracks in unusual forms under seismic pressures. Hexagonal pillars, *meshushim* in Hebrew, have created the walls of the Meshushim Pool, one of the most popular hikers' destinations in the Golan.

Whitewater rafting in the mountainous portion of the Jordan

The Jordan River

The Jordan River is 370 kilometers long from its starting point in springs at the base of Mount Hermon to the table-shaped marl mounds on the northern coast of the Dead Sea. For most of its length, the Jordan wends its way through the valley of the same name. The northern Jordan Valley is a fertile plain dotted with fishponds, citrus and mango groves. Evidence of early human existence has been discovered, in the form of primitive tools and the bones of the huge now-extinct mammals.

Clearly, early man appreciated the fertility of this region. So did third century Rabbi Simeon Ben Lakish who praised the Beit She'an Valley, through which the northern portion of the Jordan River runs, with these words: "The Garden of Eden is in the Land of Israel, and its entrance is at Beit She'an"

The character of the landscape changes as the Jordan descends towards the Dead Sea. The land becomes increasingly barren except where man-made or natural oases allow for cultivation. The river digs itself ever more deeply into the valley, meandering at some points nearly into oxbow lakes. Finally, east of Jericho the wilderness takes over completely, as the Jordan spills into the Dead Sea.

The tropical Jordan Valley

View of the River Jordan's exit from the Sea of Galilee

Beit Alpha

An inscription dates the laying of the exquisite mosaic floor at the Beit Alpha Synagogue discovered at Kibbutz Heftziba to the early sixth century CE. The floor, with one panel depicting the Holy of Holies and other salient Jewish symbols, and another depicting the offering of Isaac flanking the wheel of the Zodiac—an intriguing multicultural mix—must have been the pride of the Jewish community that once lived here. The excavation of the floor, carried out in 1929, was the first by Jewish archaeologists of an ancient synagogue in the Holy Land.

Belvoir

The crusading Hospitaller knights built a Belvoir, whose name means "beautiful view" in French, to guard the important Jordan Valley road below. In 1189, a year and a half after Muslim warrior Saladin had vanquished the Crusader Latin Kingdom of Jerusalem, Belvior stood strong. Finally, its 400 besieged defenders had no choice but to surrender. As a tribute to their endurance, Saladin allowed them to depart with their weapons for the Crusader stronghold at Tyre.

The Beit She'an theater seated some 7000.

Magnificent stone carvings graced Beit She'an's public buildings in the Roman era.

Roman-Byzantine Beit She'an-Scythopolis extends south of the ancient biblical tel.

Beit She'an

Beit She'an, like most ancient towns, was born where a river and a road converged. The river is Nahal Harod, that flows towards the Jordan from the west, and the road is the main thoroughfare linking the Jezreel Valley with the highlands of Gilead to the east.

By the time Saul fought the Philistines at nearby Mount Gilboa, Beit She'an, established by the Egyptians and named in honor of one of their deities, was a significant presence in the region, straddling an important north-south artery as well. The Bible relates that after Saul's death the Philistines "put his armor in the temple of the Ashtaroth and fastened his body to the walls of Beth She'an" (1 Sam 31:10).

After the Greeks possessed the land, the town became known as Scythopolis, in honor of the Scythian guards who mythology says protected Dionysus, patron deity of the city and god of wine. Scythopolis was one of the Decapolis towns (Mark 5:20), an alliance of cities on both sides of the Jordan. During the Roman period the town grew to become one of the largest in Palestine, and when Christianity took over the empire, it expanded even further. And then, one January day in the year 749, an earthquake felled the town. In the ensuing years, political changes in the region consigned Beit She'an to near-oblivion. Only recently has excavation and reconstruction of this city, known as "the Pompeii of Israel" ,allowed its toppled glory to return and astound the world.

A colonnaded street of Byzantine Beit She'an

The Samaritans

Numbering only a few hundred, the Samaritans are the world's smallest ethnic group. The origin of the Samaritan people stretches back to the year 721 BCE, when they were brought in to the country by King Shalmaneser, after his invasion of the northern kingdom, to replace the Israelites whom he had exiled (2 Kings:17: 6). Attacks by lions, says the Bible, were God's punishment because the newcomers did not know the Israelite faith.

The religious practices of this new faith diverged from those of the Israelites. The spiritual center of the new people became Mount Gerizim, near Shechem in Samaria, the "mountain of blessing" of Deuteronomy 27:12. As the Samaritan woman who gave Jesus water to drink at Jacob's Well noted "Our fathers worshipped in this mountain, and ye say that in Jerusalem is the place where men ought to worship" (John 4:20).

Historically, tension often prevailed between the two peoples. In the time of Ezra and Nehemiah, when Samaritans asked to participate in the rebuilding of the Temple, they were rebuffed (Ezra 4:1-4). Jesus used the example of a "good Samaritan" in a famous parable (Luke 10: 30-37). Most of his listeners would have been surprised at the notion, because of the strained relations between the two groups.

The Samaritan faith does not recognize the elucidation of biblical commandments contained in the Talmud, known as the Oral Law. They do, however, adhere strictly to biblical law. They live in two communities, one in Holon south of Tel Aviv, and the other on the slopes of Mount Gerizim, overlooking the city of Shechem. Here the Samaritan community observes Passover by sacrificing paschal lambs precisely according to Scripture.

Celebration of Samaritan Passover

Sebastia

Built over the remains of Samaria, one of the most important cities of the biblical northern kingdom of Israel, the city was embellished by Herod the Great. Even in its ruined state, its colonnaded streets, theater, and numerous other remains attenst to its charms. Ever on the lookout for a way to curry favor with his patron Caesar Augustus, Herod named the city Sebastia, which means "Augustus" in Greek.

Samaria landscape

Temple to Augustus

Ruins of a Roman-era street in Sebastia

The Negev

Israel's Arid South

The Negev is the essential land link between the Mediterranean Sea and Arabia. It is often mistakenly termed the "Negev Desert", yet not once in the 110 times it is mentioned in Scripture do these words occur together! Many parts of this vast area are barren, it is true, but it was not always so.

Psalm 126:4 reveals that water is not as absent in this region as might be imagined: "Return us O Lord, like streams in the Negev". The Bible hints at the fertility of the land in other passages, too: "Isaac sowed in that land, and received in the same year a hundred-fold" (Gen. 26:12). The secret of success in cultivating this region is knowing how to conserve the water. And two thousand years ago there existed a people who perfected this knowledge—the Nabateans.

From their capital at Petra in Edom the Nabateans administered a far-flung empire based on treasures only kings could afford: frankincense and myrrh harvested from the spice fields of Arabia. Caravans thousands of camels long bore them across the Negev to the Mediterranean, on their way to lucrative foreign markets. And only the dams and reservoirs, channels and aqueducts the Nabateans constructed allowed them to move from caravanserai to wayside station across the vast emptiness. And when the caravanserais became towns, when the Nabateans lost their independence to the Romans when they learned how to farm the land, when they became Christian and began to serve pilgrims plying the ancient roads, the magic word was, and still is, "water".

View from the Meishar Observatory

Be'er Sheva

Abraham first settled here near a water well that became a point of contention between him and King Abimelech. But Abraham was prepared to swear to the fact that he had dug the well with a gift—a time-honored way of ensuring the friendship of an adversary. Abraham named the place Be'er Sheva, the well of the oath, and planted a tamarisk tree on the spot.

Isaac, too, came here seeking water. In a strange echo of the experience of his father Abraham, he too entered into conflict with local herdsmen, concluding a treaty that ensured him access to the wells he had dug.

Archaeologists have determined that the first city wall of Be'er Sheva was constructed during the time of David or Solomon. Clearly, Solomon understood the strategic importance of this spot, gateway from the south to the highlands of Judah. And the Bible says "And Judah and Israel dwelt safely, every man under his vine and under his fig tree, from Dan even to Be'er Sheva" (1 Kings 4:25).

After almost three millennia of decline, Be'er Sheva, now gateway to Israel's south and a vibrant city of 100,000, flourishes again.

The Negev Brigade Memorial

The traditional "Abraham's Well"
Insert: The Bedouin Market

Be'er Sheva, capital of the Negev

The Bedouin

The indigenous dwellers of the deserts of the Middle East take their very name from the arid lands in which they live: badu means "desert". The intricacies of Bedouin culture allowed them to master a land whose dry climate deterred settlement by others. Few of Israel's 175,000 Bedouin still live as their forefathers did—most have abandoned their tents, flocks, and migratory life-style for permanent dwellings and a daily wage. Still, much of their traditional life-style persists.

Many aspects of Bedouin life are an inalienable part of Arab culture. One of the words in Arabic for family, for example, is ahal - tent. Indeed, family, tribe and clan are one of the most important values of Bedouin culture. In the resource-poor desert, tribal boundaries, within which are vital springs and oases, are clearly drawn and jealously guarded. Traditionally, during periods of migration, a family can leave possessions not needed on the journey in a bundle tied to trees considered their own—sometimes for months—and they will not be touched until their return!

But Bedouin do not ignore non-family members or strangers. On the contrary, extending a helping hand to a stranger (a value demonstrated in the Bible by Abraham the Patriarch, himself a desert chieftain) could be a matter of life or death for a Bedouin. Hospitality is offered with no questions asked for a limited period of time—the anonymity of the stranger protects him in case host and guest are discovered to be members of enemy tribes.

The few Bedouin that still live in goat-hair tents woven by their women, leading their sheep and goats daily to pasture and conducting their lives according to rules seemingly unchanged since the days of the Patriarchs, arouse the curiosity of all who encounter them.

Denizens of the Desert

View of Ovdat

Ovdat

Named for a deified Nabatean king, Oboda, Ovdat was founded in the fourth century BCE as a wayside station on Petra-Gaza road. When the Nabatean empire was absorbed by the Romans in the first century CE, the inhabitants of Ovdat continued to worship their old god, renaming him Zeus out of consideration for their new masters. Trade routes remained active, and the city continued to prosper. Cultivation of the surrounding areas increased; Ovdat also served as a base of military operations for the region's Roman defense lines. With the advent of Christianity, two churches were built at Ovdat, their clergy serving pilgrims plying the roads leading to and from Sinai.

Ovdat Spring

Kibbutz Sde Boker

Kibbutz Sde Boker, founded in 1952, was home in his later years to David Ben-

David Ben-Gurion

Gurion, Israel's first Prime Minister. It is said that the small agricultural community was hesitant to accept such an illustrious and world famous personality as a member, for fear his presence would disrupt their modest collective life style! But Ben-Gurion wanted to realize in his own life what he had expounded to others, that in the Negev was the future of the State of Israel and it must be inhabited. Both David Ben-Gurion, who died in 1973, and his wife, Paula, are buried close to the kibbutz, overlooking the magnificent dry riverbed of Nahal Tzin, one of "the Old Man's" favorite landscapes.

Overlooking the Negev's unique Ramon Crater

Grave of Paula and David Ben-Gurion

The dry riverbed of Nahal Tzin slices through the central Negev.

The Arava

The Arava is the southernmost part of the Israeli portion of the Syrian-African Rift. Like the rest of this 6,500 kilometer-long cleft in the earth's surface, since time immemorial the Arava has been a passageway for humans and animals migrating between Africa, Asia, and Europe. Many of the animals that once inhabited the region have become extinct but efforts are being made to restore them. The Hai-Bar Nature Reserve in the sparsely populated Arava is the perfect environment to foster the reintroduction of indigenous species.

Nature sculptures: sandstone meets limestone in the Timna Geological Park

Solomon's Pillars

The magnificent russet sandstone columns known as Solomon's Pillars do seem to have been carved at the bidding of a great king. But they are entirely, marvelously, the work of nature—wind and water shaped these exceptional formations over the millennia. Their presence did not go unnoticed by the ancient Egyptians who worked the nearby copper mines in the Late Bronze Age. A shrine where they may have worshipped was discovered at the base of the pillars.

High above it, delicately etched into the sandstone, is a drawing of the Egyptian goddess Hathor, patroness of the mines. Solomon's Pillars, the shrine and numerous rock drawings can be seen while touring the Timna Park.

Amram's Pillars

Solomon's Pillars

Nearly extinct biblical animals have been restored to their natural habitat at the Hai Bar Animal Reserve north of Eilat

ibex

ostriches

Flowers of the desert

Somali wild asses

Addax

Asiatic wild ass

Eilat

Today's Eilat was once known as Etzion Gaber, a port in the days of King Solomon. It was here that the Queen of Sheba first set foot on the soil of Israel on her way to test the legendary wisdom of the king. If the queen were to return today, she would not be ashamed to live at any one of a number of luxury hotels that now hug the shoreline between the cobalt sea and the craggy mountains of this uniquely beautiful region.

Eilat is Israel's playground. Whether camping under the stars or living the high life, visitors can enjoy Eilat's year-round sunshine and warm waters, together with some of the richest coral reefs in the world.

The Eilat Marina

Eilat, looking east towards the Gulf of Eilat and the Jordanian city of Aqaba

The Dolphin Reef
Swimming with dolphins has become a favorite pastime among Elilat vacationers.

The Gulf of Eilat

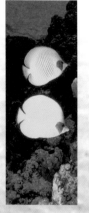

The Gulf of Eilat, is part of the Syrian African Rift, and the northwestern "arm" of the Red Sea. Some 16 miles wide, it is over 600 feet deep at its deepest point. The extraordinary reefs of the Gulf of Eilat support hundreds of species of coral and about a thousand species of fish (including forty species of shark!), making it a prime diving location.

The Underwater Observatory
Marine Park, Eilat

Eilat's spectacular corals, fish, and other living underwater treasures are on display at the famed Coral World. Among its many attractions, the underwater observatory, aquarium complex, and shark pool show off the incredible variety of marine life in the Eilat Gulf.

St. Catherine
Monastery

St. Catherine's Monastery

Still inhabited by a small number of Greek Orthodox monks, St. Catherine's Monastery was founded by Byzantine Emperor Justinian in 530 at the base of traditional Mount Sinai where Moses received the Ten Commandments. In addition to its chapel, church, and "skull room", where the remains of long-deceased monks are laid to rest, the monastery boasts a library which contains thousands of rare documents.

St. Catherine's bell-tower

The skull room

Rooftops within St. Catherine's walls

Bedouin in the vicinity of Mount Sinai converted to Christianity in the Byzantine era.

Petra's Cardo and gateway to Qasr el-Bint

Jordan

Like other countries in the region, the Hashemite Kingdom of Jordan was once part of the Ottoman Empire and was created by a series of Great Power moves in the region in the wake of World War 1. Its vast area is populated by some four and a half million people, about fifty per cent of whom live in its capital, Amman and its other main cities, Irbid, Zarka, and its attractive Red Sea port city, Aqaba. Over half the population is composed of Palestinian refugees from the region's wars. In 1995, Jordan, now ruled by King Abdullah II, son of the late King Hussein, signed a peace treaty with Israel and opened its borders, greatly increasing tourist traffic between the two nations.

Petra

Petra, in southwestern Jordan, is Jordan's prime tourist destination. Known as Sela in the Bible, it was the capital of the land of Edom. But Petra's heydey came when the Nabateans, ancient masters of the spice route linking Arabia with the the Mediterranean, both fortified and beautified it. Later, the Romans and finally the Byzantine Christians also embellished the town and its environs. Visitors to Petra marvel at the remains of the city and the tombs of its wealthy citizens cut from the famed red rock, and dramatically revealed at the end of the narrow canyon known as the "Siq".

Qasr el-Bint

Index